ACCOUNTING
1, 2, 3
FOR BUSY BUSINESS OWNERS

Take Charge of your Accounting and
Really Run Your Business Profitably!

MARIE GIBSON
Managerial Consultant & Award winning Educator

Books published by Marie Gibson Management & Consulting LLC are available at special discounts for bulk purchases by corporations, institutions and other organizations. For more information, please contact the publisher.

Marie Gibson Management & Consulting LLC
PO Box 17323
Reno, NV 89511

Visit our Web site at www.marie-gibson.com

ISBN: 978-0-9843774-0-4

Interior design by Ponderosa Pine Design, Vicky Vaughn Shea

Illustrations by ©2009 Jupiterimages Corporation and Drashya Designs

Printed in the United States of America

Second Edition

Acknowledgements

I would like to thank a number of my clients, students, friends, mentors and family, to each of whom I am truly grateful. I appreciate each of my students and clients who have allowed me to work with them and who have helped me improve my ability to explain accounting processes and systems in a simple and easy-to-understand manner.

I'd like to thank the Nevada Small Business Development Center, the University of Nevada Reno, SCORE volunteers, Western Nevada College, Morrison University, Lake Tahoe Community College, as well as others who provided to me great opportunities to teach and share my knowledge with business owners and students.

The original book would never have been written without Meggin McIntosh, who encouraged me to quit talking about it and write it. I thank my niece, Amanda, who provided great insights into what made sense in the written word, and I thank my friends, Rosana Halprine and Elaine McNeill, who provided editing services.

I'd especially like to thank my sister Lynn Gibson, who took me white-water rafting—resulting in a broken ankle that allowed me time to finish the original work that summer. And a special thank-you for my dear husband, Dave Archer, who, with great patience, encouraged me to finish my "story-telling" so that others may understand the benefits of accurate financial reporting!

My thanks and appreciation to all of you!

Table of Contents

Introduction

Welcome to **ACCOUNTING 1, 2, 3 FOR BUSY BUSINESS OWNERS.** You have taken the essential step of running your business for profit: managing and understanding your accounting so you can make better decisions that drive your business to grow and thrive; not just survive!

This book provides an easy and simple to understand formula for getting your accounting system in order. It provides step-by-step instructions you can apply immediately to help you through the hurdles of setting up your accounting system correctly, understanding your reports and creating financial statements so you can make better business decisions. When an accounting system is created properly, your transactions flow into your records; these records flow into your reports; and you can use your reports for your ultimate business goal: increased profit. Imagine, timely and accurate financial statements that you can finally understand and know how to use to improve your business' bottom line!

This book is for you if you are a business owner or manager, if you are planning to launch a business or if you are the manager of a not-for-profit organization, and ...

- ☑ you're feeling lost and overwhelmed by your accounting,
- ☑ you have no clue how the figures get into the reports,
- ☑ you're confused about what records you should keep and how long you should keep them,
- ☑ your office desk is piled high with paperwork,
- ☑ you don't want to look at or deal with another number,
- ☑ you are spending a fortune on professional accounting fees,
- ☑ you are unable to use your reports for wise decision-making.

You are not alone! Many entrepreneurs, directors and managers love running a business or non-profit organization–the creative side, the people part, the new technology, the marketing aspects– but they cannot stand the thought of accounting and paperwork. It leaves them anxious, confused and defeated before they even begin. Paper paralysis sets in and their offices become burdened with ever-building piles that impact productive workflow.

ACCOUNTING 1, 2, 3 FOR BUSY BUSINESS OWNERS is presented in layperson language with easy-to-understand explanations, recommendations and illustrations. It shows you how to:

- ☑ Set up a simple, inexpensive, hassle-free accounting system.
- ☑ Utilize software programs to streamline your systems and protect your vital information.
- ☑ Interview and select qualified accountants to assist with the more complex aspects of accounting and taxation.
- ☑ Understand your reports for business decision-making.
- ☑ Create a budget that works for your company and allows you to thrive.
- ☑ Prepare necessary records for governmental and other business purposes.

My clients have successfully implemented my unique and innovative method of teaching accounting. As I began setting up financial records and systems for business owners and managers, I learned that they didn't understand the basics of accounting–they found it just too confusing. Most knew that they needed to save all their documentation; and save it they did ... usually in a shoebox or accumulated on the corner shelf. Maybe if they ignored it, it would magically transform itself into a neat and tidy system with reports that they could read and understand. Never happened!

My clients range from small businesses to mid-size companies and not-for-profit organizations. Some business owners have started their businesses as a hobby and never paid much attention to the numbers. Other business owners have backgrounds in corporate business. It doesn't seem to matter. Even professionals that are fully competent in their chosen fields are likely to be overwhelmed by their lack of basic level accounting knowledge that allows them to keep life simple! Because they are professionals who have managed large corporate budgets they are sometimes embarrassed that they don't know how to take charge of their own records in setting up a system.

The root problem is that many business owners find their accounting systems are like a foreign language—or a foreign country—and will take extra effort. In the past, would purchase a number of books for my clients, hoping to find one that could explain the procedures in a down-to-earth manner for business owners. Most of what I found was written by accounting people for accounting people; not truly helpful for the business owners. Thus, the creation of this book—a back-to-basics accounting book **written by a business owner for business owners**, managers and directors. It is titled **ACCOUNTING 1, 2, 3 FOR BUSY BUSINESS OWNERS**! because that is exactly what I will teach you. Creating a smart accounting system leads directly to making smart business decisions, thus improving your profitability.

This book provides you with something real, something basic, and something applicable in your fast-paced world. You will learn how to set up your accounting system at the foundational level. This initial creation affects your chart of accounts, and how your chart of accounts is set up affects your business reports. Ultimately these reports affect your business decisions and your ability to make good decisions determines if you can survive and thrive in these tough economic times. **ACCOUNTING 1, 2, 3 FOR BUSY BUSINESS OWNERS**!

It doesn't matter whether you are using a manual system or a computerized system. It doesn't matter if you are doing the books or hiring an employee or contractor to help you. It is important for you to understand how the accounting system flows and use these concepts to create reports that you can rely on. It is the job of

ACCOUNTING 1, 2, 3 FOR BUSY BUSINESS OWNERS to help you understand this flow and to take charge of your accounting system—simply!

Your adventure starts in the first chapter where you'll see how an accounting system can be easy and effective, and why it is important to you and your business.

Chapter 2, *Let's Dive Right In!* lays the foundation for your accounting system. You want a solid base when you create your accounting system. It should be basic and give you information you need to build your business.

In Chapter 3, *Understanding and Loving Your Chart of Accounts,* you'll learn how to organize your system so that you're speaking the same language as other successful businesses—using standardized records and reports to effectively and accurately communicate.

Chapter 4, *Taking Charge—Tools For Cash Flow,* describes the essential tasks required for keeping track of your money as it comes in and goes out of your business.

Chapter 5, *Financial Reports—How to Create Good Ones,* shows you how your transactions flow into your Profit & Loss report, your Balance Sheet and your Cash Flow Statement. With these reports, you will learn to understand and fine-tune the performance of your business.

Chapter 6, *Your Newest, Best Friend,* provides you with suggestions for interviewing and hiring accountants when you need help with your books. This chapter also introduces basic accounting terminology so that you can learn to speak the same language.

In Chapter 7, you learn *Everything You Didn't Want to Know About Taxes—And More*! This chapter discusses sales tax, use tax, Federal self-employment tax and payroll taxes and includes a section on self-employed, independent contractors.

Chapter 8, *A Two-Second Click,* guides you through the decision of computerizing your manual accounting system and includes a section on embezzlement protection.

Chapter 9, *Odds 'N' Ends,* includes several topics that are concerns to business owners: handling deposits and down payments, bartering, depreciation and accrual basis versus cash basis accounting.

Chapter 10, *Budgeting For Profit*, is a must-read for owners that have, up until now, avoided budgeting.

I'm looking forward to helping you with your adventure through **ACCOUNTING 1, 2, 3 FOR BUSY BUSINESS OWNERS** so that you too can take control of your accounting and run your business for fun and profit!

Warm regards—*Marie Gibson*

P.S. There are no debits and credits in this book!

Getting Ready For Your Journey

Through ACCOUNTING 1, 2, 3
FOR BUSY BUSINESS OWNERS

Your journey through **ACCOUNTING 1, 2, 3 FOR BUSY BUSINESS OWNERS** will help you understand how a basic accounting system should be created, how to record transactions, and how to keep track of your income and expenses, your customers, vendors and your employees. You'll create a system using a Chart of Accounts, learn why it is the central hub or part of your financial accounting and watch as your transactions flow through the mapping provided by your Chart of Accounts directly into your reports. You'll become empowered and acquire the ability to create and read primary accounting reports. With a properly designed accounting system, your business can flourish. You can take charge of your money, and you can really run your business profitably!

Often the owner or manager of a small business or not-for-profit organization performs all the recordkeeping, bookkeeping and accounting activities—sometimes with minimal assistance. Some owners choose to hire out their bookkeeping and accounting functions due to time constraints, lack of interest or lack of ability. These owners and managers must still learn enough to protect their business, read reports regularly, ask appropriate questions regarding the finances of the business and be able to use the financial records to run their business for fun and profit! Sometimes the terms *recordkeeping, bookkeeping and accounting* are used interchangeably so it's important to take a look at definitions and distinctions.

Recordkeeping is the process of creating a system to store necessary documents–financial as well as non-financial. It's the process of filing and keeping all your records in a manner enabling you to locate information that you need in a timely fashion. There are all kinds of records that are not financially related–for example, copies of your lease documents, insurance policies and previous claims, advertising and collateral files, presentations and speeches, notes on research, and vendor catalogs. A good recordkeeping system enables you to find these documents quickly and easily.

Bookkeeping is the basic tracking and recording of all financial transactions by using a standard procedure that was developed in 1494 by an Italian monk to keep his employees honest. Cash coming into a business (income, investments and loans) and money going out of a business (expenses, purchase of assets and other payments) is called cash flow. It is important to record these transactions and to keep track of them for a multitude of reasons. As your business grows, you will find that you'll need the summary of these transactions on a regular basis to talk the same language as other business professionals.

Accounting is more analytical in nature, and includes the areas of taxation, audit, financial statement analysis, and decision-making based on review of the records and is referred to as managerial accounting. Professional accountants study for years, passing classes, taking specialized exams, interning and ultimately becoming either a certified public accountant or a certified management accountant. I'll discuss accountants, other accounting services and reports in detail in Chapter Six.

There are generally two types of accounting, although some of the functions overlap.

Financial accounting is generally for the preparation and sharing of your business information with business outsiders– governmental authorities, shareholders and lenders. The reports are created with these purposes in mind.

Managerial accounting is for internal decision-making so that you can make wise decisions about your business–usually to make more money!

Reasons for Keeping Financial Records

There are several primary reasons for keeping records of your financial transactions. Consider your financial records a form of story-telling; story-telling that shares the story of your business' health with yourself and others. The "story" is written in a manner which can be understood . . . . We want our stories to say that our business is profitable!

Income tax records–You must maintain records that allow your accountant to prepare your Federal and state income tax returns. This is indeed a truly important reason for keeping records. You need records showing your income and expenses so that your accountant can create your income tax returns on an annual basis. If you give your accountant your 'shoebox' filled with messy papers, it won't be free. You will be charged for simply organizing that box of papers and recording basic transactions. One of the easiest ways to reduce your annual accounting fees is to organize your own system.

Borrowing money–If you plan to borrow money from investors or bankers, you will need to present your financial records for review. Normally, you would provide an income statement, balance sheet, and tax returns for three years, as well as other projections and budgets on how you plan to pay back the loan with interest. **ACCOUNTING 1, 2, 3 FOR BUSY BUSINESS OWNERS** shows you how these financial statements are created from your records.

Keeping track of your cash flow–Whether it's coming in or going out, you'll need to keep an eye on your money, especially during economic downturns. When you understand your cash flow, you know if you owe money to others and whether others owe you payments for the purchase of your goods and services. If you have customers that owe you money, you can track those and request and collect payments regularly—this is called an Accounts Receivable list. If you have vendors and suppliers that you owe money, you'll track those to make sure you pay them when the bill is due—this is an Accounts Payable list. By implementing a simple system, you can eliminate late fees for delinquent payments made to suppliers. Late fees of any kind are a warning that your system isn't working well for you, and there is seldom a good reason for having them assessed.

Profitability—Another primary reason that you need to keep records is to determine the profitability of the business—are you making money? And, if not, what should be changed? Are you spending a lot of money on non-income producing items? New business owners need to learn the skill of evaluating every dollar they spend and ask themselves, "What is this dollar's anticipated return to the business? How much will this expenditure make for me in terms of dollars?" In other words, "How much income will be created by spending this money?" The use of your internal records for decision-making is called managerial accounting. For instance, expensive office furniture may be nice (and yes, it may be necessary in some industries), but it's probably not what's producing the income initially. Think carefully about the dollars you spend and where you will get the most return or income for your money.

Creating a Good System

A good system will track the money going into and out of your business. This is called cash flow and it is always important to know if your business has enough money—not only to pay its bills, but also to have extra left over. Can you expand? Are you able to hire employees to help? After all of your hard work, can you take money out of the business? Cash flow reports provide this information and help you understand the timing of your cash flows. For instance, if part of the year you have excess cash coming in and other parts of the year you have excess cash going out, you need to plan for a shortage at that certain time.

Keeping good records helps you to know and understand your customers, individually and as a group. Your records will show which clients or customers are the most profitable. When you have good records, you can filter your customers and offer something specifically for a smaller group. Also, if a current customer is pleased with your service and products, it is easier to market and sell to them repeatedly, rather than finding and obtaining new customers.

By having good records, you'll be able to apply for credit with vendors and suppliers. Many of them provide goods and services 'on account' or 'on credit' after reviewing your financial records. A supplier who processes your application for an account with him (this is called net terms) is trying to determine if your business is legitimate, if you are financially viable and if they should trust you to pay. Often, you will conduct business with these vendors for a period of several months with shipments coming to you in a manner known as COD (cash on delivery). Once your vendors know and trust you to pay, you may be allowed to apply for terms. They will ask you to fill out an application or provide your financial statements for their review. 'Net 30' is very common and means that your payment must be received by the vendor within thirty days. Some vendors encourage your payment by providing discounts if paid early. For instance, you may be offered 2% 10, Net 30. This vendor is offering you a two percent discount if the payment is RECEIVED within ten days. If you do not pay within the ten days, the net (full) payment is due by the thirtieth day. You should plan to mail checks or create online payments early enough so that the payment is received on time.

A good system will provide accurate records to report your income, expenses, and payroll properly for Federal and state taxation purposes. Some businesses keep extremely accurate records of their income, and yet they are unable to find all the receipts for their expenses. Your business (or you) depending on your legal entity, pays income taxes on the 'net' income. This is the difference between your income and your expenses. If you can't find your expense documentation, you'll pay higher income taxes. There is no bluffing–if you are ever audited by the government, you need the physical receipts and the proper records.

A good accounting system will help you when you need to apply for a loan as you grow and expand. Most banks, credit unions, angel investors and micro-lending organizations wish to see current financial statements and tax returns for the past two to three years. They will also request proforma (expected) budget statements for the next two to three years, specifically looking for the business's ability to pay back the loan. All these financials need to be as accurate as possible to reflect the financial position of the business.

You need to make informed decisions regarding the price of your products and services. A well-designed system will provide accurate financial records quickly so you know how to fine-tune your business. As a new business owner, you may price your services and products too high and they don't sell, or you may price them too low and you're not making a profit. Your profitability reports for your business, your specific jobs and your clients help you with these insights.

A good system provides records and reports for:
- Tracking money in and out
- Applying for credit with vendors and suppliers
- Knowing and understanding your customers
- Federal and state taxation purposes
- Applying for a loan
- Decisions regarding the pricing of your products and services, thus influencing your profitability.

Terminology

Using the appropriate terms when you discuss your business' finance with others indicates that you are a professional and are determined to learn proper accounting procedures, standardized reporting and can tell the story of your business properly. I begin with a few basic words and continue to discuss terminology throughout the book. You'll want your system to ultimately answer the following questions quickly and accurately.

How much money am I bringing in?	Sales Revenue
How much am I spending?	Expenses and Assets
Is my business making any money?	Net Income (Sales Revenue-Expenses)
Which jobs/customers/clients are profitable?	Profitability report
What's the value of what my business owns?	Assets
How much does my business owe to others?	Accounts Payables (A/P), other current liabilities, credit cards, loans
How much do others owe to my business?	Accounts Receivables (A/R), loans to others
What is my business worth?	Net worth

As a business owner, using the terminology helps you become comfortable with the concepts. The more comfortable you are, the more confident you will be in turning your story into wise business decisions!

Enough talk; Let's Dive Right In!

Let's Dive Right In!

Setting Up Your Accounting System

What You Need to Start with the Basics

It is imperative that you organize your records into a system so that your reports will be in a standardized form allowing for easy reading and interpreting. This standardization process provides a language that is customary in financial statements. As well-known businessman Warren Buffett says, "accounting is the language of business." Just like we use letters, words, sentences, paragraphs and chapters when we write a story-book, we will use numbers, transactions and reports to tell the story of how our business is doing.

Your initial recordkeeping and bookkeeping system should be simple. As your business grows so will your accounting system. So don't worry—you don't have to anticipate every possible transaction or potential scenario that might occur in the future. I have found that most new businesses shift, add, edit, delete, and merge components of their system over the course of several months as they determine which features are important to them. Your initial goal is to create an easily accessible system of information that meets the everyday needs of your operation. If the system you design is not simple and easy-to-use, you probably won't use it; and if you do use it, you may become frustrated and confused.

The concepts in this book apply to creating both manual and computerized systems. Sometimes business owners start using accounting software without any understanding of how the system should be created and create chaos for themselves. The journey through **ACCOUNTING 1, 2, 3 FOR BUSY BUSINESS OWNERS** provides steps that assume that you are creating a manual system and that computer financial software will be adopted in the future when needed. As your business or your non-profit organization grows, you will find that having financial software such as Simple Start®, Quicken®, Peachtree® or QuickBooks® will be inevitable and desirable. Any of these will save you an immense amount of time and will insure mathematical accuracy. We'll discuss accounting software in Chapter 8.

Creating files–The first step in creating a manual accounting system is to buy inexpensive file folders to file your paperwork and records. These can be found at an office supply store, a local pharmacy or a large discount store. Buy the least expensive, plain manila folders with tabs. The name tabs are the little extra part at the top of the folder, and you can find the folders with the name tabs located on the left, the right and the center areas. You might like to purchase a combination package where the folders have the name tabs located in each of the three positions–some to the left, some in the center and some to the right. These make locating label headings easier when you are trying to find a folder in your file cabinet. Avoid spending money on a specialty system when you're first getting started. As your business or non-profit expands and you are able to critique different specialty systems, you may find something you like better. But for now, let's just get started.

For the headings that are on the tabs, some people like to purchase color-coded labels or marking pens. When your headings are in colors and define your folders visually, it's easier to find them quickly–although you may not have that many folders initially. You will be adding folders later and can always add colors later. Remember, it is not necessary to have your system created for the next umpteen years. Start with what you have and grow from there. You may have less than a dozen file folders to begin, and that's perfectly fine.

You also need a file cabinet or other container to hold your file folders. This could be anything from a cardboard box, a plastic file box, an old delivery milk carton, and a two-drawer cabinet to a four-drawer cabinet. And, yes, many people use a shoebox or a boot box. If you plan to locate this cabinet where it's visible to the public, you want to invest in one that is high quality and looks nice. If you are short on cash and tempted to purchase a cheap metal cabinet, you may not like it. You might consider using a couple of plastic file boxes until you can purchase a decent file cabinet. You may also wish to have a combination of file boxes: one for storage in the office, one close to your desk for daily neatness and one for travel.

To start preparing your file folders, you'll create a few generic and basic headings. Start with labels that indicate various types of purchases. Everyone's files will ultimately be a little different– there are no wrong headings. For example, you might start with the following headings: rent, telephone, utilities, insurance, travel, offices supplies, advertising and so forth.

You want to organize your transactions into types of transactions, **not by month**. Avoid using monthly headings such as January, February, March, etc. for your file folders in a business setting. The organization of your file folders is similar to the organization of your chart of accounts and thus, ultimately, your reports and financial statements. It is this organization that leads to the standardization of your financial reports.

It is imperative that you separate your personal financial transactions from your business transactions. Physically separate your business file folders from any of your personal file folders–don't just separate them in your mind. Maintaining this physical division reiterates the importance of separating your records for personal and business as well, and makes it easier to find records. As an aside, if your business is ever subject to an IRS audit, separate records will make your life much smoother. If you have mixed or co-mingled your personal and business records, the auditor may request to see all of them.

Use as many file folders as you need to keep your paperwork organized, but not so many that they become cumbersome. To determine whether you need additional file folders, ask yourself, "How will keeping this information in a separate folder help me to manage and grow my business?" For instance, do you need three separate file folders for gas, water and electric bills, or does one called 'utilities' suffice? On the other hand, if you travel extensively for your business, you may wish to have separate file folders for 'travel-motel,' 'travel-airfares' and 'travel-meals.' I suggest keeping fewer file folders to begin with and adding more as your business or non-profit grows.

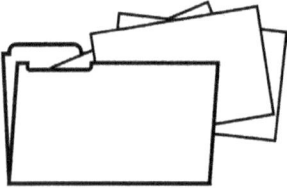

You will be organizing these file folders in a specific manner as you proceed with your journey through **ACCOUNTING 1, 2, 3 FOR BUSY BUSINESS OWNERS** but for now it is enough just to determine the names of the folders. Jot the file folders you have and/or think that you should have.

As we travel through **ACCOUNTING 1, 2, 3 FOR BUSY BUSINESS OWNERS** I occasionally explain conceptual ideas and suggest how you should perform that action. Realistically, I know that people try to shortcut even the simplest of systems. Even a shortcut must have a system, so I also provide alternate practices.

Creating Summary Sheets

Conceptually–You insert a one-page sheet of paper inside each file folder, and as you place documents, receipts and transaction records into your file folders, you'll record the transactions on the paper. Record every item that you put in the folder. This is what accountants call "recording or posting entries." At the end of each month, subtotal the items on the page so that you have a running total of the transactions in the file.

Realistically–The challenge is that sometimes there are a lot of receipts and transactions and it seems like an overwhelming task to record every transaction on that one sheet of paper, so none of it gets done. The paperwork piles up on the floor, in a closet, on a bookshelf and sometimes in the wastebasket. As an alternative to recording every transaction, you may use a calculator to add the transactions in each file folder for each month and record the summary of the monthly total on the sheet. You may also wish to use a spreadsheet to make tracking and adding easier and quicker. To keep previous monthly transactions from intermixing with the new transactions, keep them divided either with a large paperclip or inserted into an envelope. At the end of each month, the totals on the summary sheets from each file folder are transferred to the overall summary sheet.

Calculating your receipts and invoices is imperative for knowing the total income and expenses of your business, and thus your profit or loss. Preparing these records monthly should become a habit, not a chore. You will love the result–receiving feedback about your income and expenses immediately. Try to file your transactions on a regular basis. Fifteen minutes weekly doesn't seem like much–until you multiple that by 52 weeks. Yes, that would be thirteen hours…no wonder we don't always like doing it at the end of the year. If you just can't file your transactions weekly, then at a bare minimum you must spend one hour a month filing and organizing your paperwork. As your business grows, this one hour will grow.

Because this portion of bookkeeping can be tedious, many people postpone it until the end of the year and either panic and/ or pay a fortune for an accountant to organize their records and subtotal the folders. This is one area that you can easily perform yourself or with the help of an inexpensive assistant, and save several hundred dollars … well worth the money.

Sample Summary Page						
	Jan	Feb	March	April	May	June
Income						
Hourly Consulting						
Workshop Training						
Custom Projects						
E-books						
Retail Sales						
Teleseminars						
Total Income						
Expenses						
Rent						
Telephone						
Office Supplies						
Insurance						
Promos & Advertising						
Internet Service						
Professional Consulting						
Bank Service Fees						
Travel						
Meals						
Automobile						
Airfare						
Hotel						
Total Expenses						

Organization of file folders–Now we're going to discuss how your file folders should be organized in the cabinet. When learning any new game, you want to learn the rules. The organization of your financial records has rules and these rules influence the look of your financial statements. Using the rules produces standardized reports you can share with others who speak the same language. A special board issues rules for accounting. These rules are called GAAP (generally accepted accounting principles.

To begin playing the game, you initially type or write the names of all your file folders on a one-page list. Once you are finished, this list is no longer called a list–it is now called a chart of accounts and the individual names of your file folders are called 'accounts.' That's it! And, you thought accounts and a chart of accounts were more sophisticated and that it was difficult to understand!?

The challenge comes when your accountant wants you to use his/her list of standard accounts with his ready-made chart of accounts. Her list (chart of accounts) may have accounts that you don't have and you may not understand what they are. That's okay. Everyone's file folders (accounts) are different. Accountants have a rather large chart of accounts because they're trying to think of every account that any one of their clients uses and they combine everyone's accounts into one long list. They standardize the list so that it facilitates their work with clients. This doesn't mean that you should have every one of those accounts–you may only have a few when you start your business. You may add more as your business grows or your accountant asks you to create one for a specific reason.

Now, close your eyes ... we're going to do some envisioning ... we're going to organize your accounts, your file folders, in a very specific way in your chart of accounts.

Imagine that your file cabinet has five drawers–you're going to be dividing your file folders into five separate cabinet drawers. You don't actually need to buy a five-drawer cabinet; you're just going to pretend that you have

one so that you can group your file folders (now called your chart of accounts) into five major categories or types. These are the same groupings that accountants use. Even though you may not be using a five-drawer cabinet, these five groupings become very important to you, your business and your accountant as your business expands and you need to produce accurate financial statements.

You may want to use the colored labels to group your file folders into the five categories outlined below. Be bold–labels and file folders can be replaced if you put the file in the wrong grouping.

- The top drawer (category #1) is for file folders that hold papers pertaining to your **assets**–everything that your company owns.
- The second drawer (category #2) is for papers related to your business' **liabilities and debts**.
- The third drawer (category #3) should contain files pertaining to your personal, partnership and shareholder investments in the company, called **equity or capital investment**.
- The fourth drawer (category #4) is reserved for your **income** file folders.
- The fifth drawer (category #5), always the largest and thus the heaviest (so it provides a solid foundation for the cabinet), is for your **operating expenses**. We discuss each of these drawers (each of these account types) in detail throughout the next chapter.

It is imperative you organize your accounts (file folders) into the five major categories (types) used by accountants. The chart of accounts is the center of your system. It organizes your transactions so that your reports will be in a standardized form that anyone can easily read and interpret.

Next Chapter: Understanding and Loving your Chart of Accounts!

3

Understanding and Loving Your Chart of Accounts!

Assets

We transfer the idea of a five-drawer file cabinet, directly to your chart of accounts. We use the filing cabinet and the process of filing to create a permanent picture in our minds of the major groups that are used in your chart of accounts. The top drawer (category #1) is for file folders that hold papers pertaining to your business assets. Assets are everything that your company owns. An asset is usually tangible–something that you can touch. However, this account also includes the recording and tracking of intangible assets, such as copyrights, patents and trademarks. Examples of tangible assets that a company might own are cash, computers, printers, maintenance and operating equipment, desks, furnishings and your business checking and savings accounts. You want file folders for each asset. If you have multiple accounts, each of those accounts needs its own folder.

You absolutely want a separate checking account for your business–even if you are a sole proprietor. By opening a checking account in your business name, you will have an immediate mind shift indicating that you are serious about this work and earning a profit from it. A separate checking account indicates that you are a professional and

that you intend to keep your business and personal purchases separate and run your business like a business instead of a hobby. And if these reasons are not enough, it also simplifies the accounting process! Keep your bank statements and reconciliations in this file folder. Canceled checks should be organized by date, banded together and kept separately in a storage box for convenience.

Accounts Receivable–Your Accounts Receivable (A/R) list is an asset. You want a file folder for your A/R, which is a list of your customers who owe you money for goods and services that they purchased from your business. If you don't allow accounts or payment terms for your customers, you won't have A/R and thus no need for a file. If your business has loaned money to another entity with a Note Payable, a Memo of Understanding or another type of contract, it is an asset and warrants a separate folder for that loan. If somebody owes you money personally, this is not business related and thus no business file folder is needed. This may sound like nagging, but separating your personal and business funds is imperative.

Client files–You may also wish to have individual file folders for each client regardless of whether they owe you money. Keeping track of your clients' and customers' purchases and service requests provides a great deal of background history for the next time they call. I like to keep notes and records of meetings, driving directions, service visit notes, etc. in the client file folders. If you have a few customers that purchased only once from you and you have transaction documents for those times, file them into a Miscellaneous Customer file folder. You may wish to keep your permanent client files in drawer #4 (the income drawer), but either location is fine as long as your keep the system consistent.

Inventory purchases–You will want to envision keeping the records of your inventory purchases in the top cabinet drawer, listed as an asset. Inventory consists of the items that you buy with the purpose of reselling. These items are considered to be assets of the company, even if you have not yet paid for them.

Assets versus expenses–Sometimes there is a bit of a grey area when deciding whether your purchase is an asset or expense. Take office supplies, for example. Many of us correctly consider office supplies as expenses, while others properly consider them to be current assets … how can this be? Technically, they should be considered assets when they are purchased and then re-categorized as expenses once they are used. For smaller companies, this is not usually an issue. For example, office supplies are often used quickly and don't remain in the supply room long enough to be considered an asset. It's very rare for a small business to have a large inventory of office (or other) supplies at the end of their fiscal year. Begin recording office supplies as an expense. As your company grows and you begin accumulating a large inventory of surplus supplies, you may decide to treat them as an asset. Your folders (accounts) can be changed at that time.

The following documents and papers should be kept in your asset file drawer, inside the appropriate file folder:

- Purchase receipts, warranties and contact information
- Cash register tape receipts from purchases
- Credit card sales receipts
- Deposit slip receipts for your bank accounts.

Liabilities

The second drawer (category #2) is for your business liabilities. These include all debts like Accounts Payable, IOU's for money that was borrowed from your friends and family, loans from a bank or credit union and business credit cards. You'll need to create a file folder for each one of these accounts.

Accounts Payable (A/P) is a list of the money that you owe to suppliers and vendors. When you purchase inventory, the list of inventory becomes an asset and you keep a list of inventory assets in the first drawer (category #1). If you borrow the money to purchase the inventory, either through a long-term bank loan or a short-term loan from your suppliers, there is an additional file

folder in the second drawer, listing this debt as a liability. This short-term loan from your suppliers is called terms and is usually for 15, 30 or 60 days. It is important to pay these when agreed so that you can continue ordering from the company.

The process of keeping two file folders for the inventory purchase transactions may seem daunting–remember, one in assets for the inventory and one in A/P for the loan of the money to purchase the inventory. However, it's important to keep two separate folders because you may sell the inventory and still owe the loan (or sometimes, you'll pay off the loan and still own the inventory).You need to be able to track the information properly and create accurate reports.

Likewise, if you purchase another asset like equipment or an automobile by using a loan, you'll have a file folder for that asset in the first category (Assets) and you'll also want one in the liabilities drawer for the loan.

Business credit card–You'll want a credit card file folder for each business credit card. You may find it difficult to get a business credit card within the first few years of business. A credit card company will ask you to file an application for review. Sometimes, your local bank will issue a credit card for your business when you maintain a certain balance with them. If you don't have a business credit card, you'll want to obtain a separate, personal card for convenience and limit it for purchases related to your business. Again, the importance of separating your business from your personal financial records cannot be overemphasized.

Be careful not to make business purchases with your personal card; and do not make personal purchases with the business card. It is important to keep personal and business transactions separate so that you'll have a clear idea of your business performance. And, yes, if you do mix them, the world will come to a screeching halt. Maybe, not. But your accounting system will need to be fixed. You will need to 'reimburse' the appropriate card for the expenses that were incorrectly charged to it. Your accounting system can do this with a journal entry ... but we are not even talking about those yet. It is much cleaner and simpler to follow the golden rule regarding business and personal purchases. Act professionally—separate your personal and business purchases. Nag, nag, nag again. It cannot be said too much!

Note and loan payables—When you agree to borrow money from family, friends or a lender, your business has acquired a loan (a debt, a liability) and this is normally called a Note payable or a Loan payable. You want a file folder for each and this information is kept in the second drawer (the liabilities drawer).

Again, you may not have an actual file cabinet with five different drawers, but we use this visualization so you can organize and understand the GAAP accounting system for creating financial reports.

Equity/Net Worth

The third drawer (category #3) should contain files (accounts) pertaining to your personal investment in the company. This includes money and/or equipment that you give the company to start. You may also have file folders to record investments made by partners, shareholders and other investors.

Sole proprietor—If you are a sole proprietor (no legal status of incorporation), you may just give or lend the business money to get started. Sometimes there is the expectation by you or your spouse or other family members that the money invested in the company will be paid back so keep track of it. When you file Federal income taxes, using the form Schedule C for sole proprietors, the information flows directly into your personal tax records, so be careful how it's entered.

Also some people continue to invest money into the business when there is not enough money being earned and the business has bills and expenses that need to be paid. You'll want to record

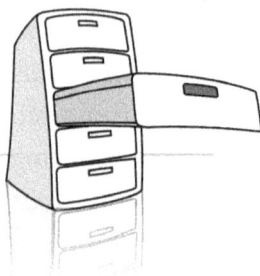

this money as an investment. Also, you don't wish to pay income tax on this invested money–it's not business income. That's why we keep separate file folders in the equity section of our system.

If the business is earning money, a sole proprietor may withdraw money from the business and this is recorded as an investment withdrawal (sometimes referred to as a draw). You'll want a separate folder for withdrawals–also called draws.

Partnership, C Corp or Limited Liability Corp (LLC)–If your business is incorporated as a Partnership, C Corp or Limited Liability Corp (LLC), the connection between personal investments and withdrawals, must be clearly distinguished from the funds of the business. A partnership and a corporation are their own legal entities and you may not just invest and withdraw money in and out of them without appropriate documentation. You need the assistance of your accountant to show you how to handle these transactions properly in your records. The full discussion regarding the legal entity of your business and the benefits of a sole proprietorship versus a corporation is worthy of a full book. You'll want to research this further and seek the advice of a business attorney.

Income

This is our fourth category and this area in your files and records is reserved for your income file folders. You may have folders for the following: consulting, retail sales, corporate training, workshops, e-books, hourly services and others. You may hesitate to keep your income sources in separate files, but after a few years, you will be glad that you started. By separating your income into different folders, you can see where you earn the most profit. You can also start determining which products and types of services are profitable, which products and services to keep and which ones don't warrant the investment of time and energy.

Eventually, you also want to start tracking which clients or customers are most profitable and which ones you may choose to decline in the future. If you have retail sales, you may wish to keep folders for the different types of goods that you sell, similar to a department store. Again, your ultimate goal is to reduce inventory that doesn't sell and maximize the investment in items that sell repeatedly. A good accounting system will provide this information.

I like to keep my individual client file folders in the drawer and use them to record details about clients and any information that may help me when I speak with them next. When you have only a few customers, your memory will serve you fine. As you acquire additional clients, you'll need to jot notes. It only took one reminder for me. I felt compelled to 'write off' a visit with a client. I needed to duplicate a repair to her system that I had previously made and I hadn't kept any notes from the first visit. I had to spend time reconfiguring what I forgot.

You will wish to keep copies of receipts that you have written for your clients. These can be placed into their folders after you have noted the income on your summary sheet that is located in the front of each file folder. You also want to keep copies of any estimates and bids that haven't been accepted. You can refer to them for future estimates and billings and not have to start from scratch each time you are preparing another estimate. Remember, your separate A/R (Accounts Receivable) list showing which customers owe you money? It will have its own file in the asset category.

If you are a retail store, *conceptually* you will keep your daily cash register tapes and your daily credit

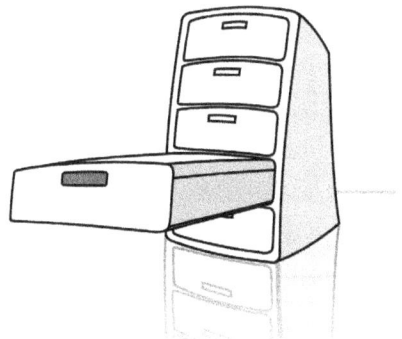

card batch in this category. *Realistically*, the paperwork becomes cumbersome quickly and you'll want to obtain some office storage boxes. Here's a system that works well: place your daily documents, including the register tapes, batch statements and the daily drawer reconciliation form, into a #10 envelope. On the outside, mark the day of the week and the date and place the envelopes in sequential order in the storage box. When you need to research a specific transaction, they'll be easy to find.

For many consultants and service providers, your clients will send you a 1099-Miscellaneous Form at the end of the year showing how much they paid you. These forms are necessary for accurate tax calculations. Your clients must create them for unincorporated contractors whom they paid more than $600 to, within one year. Even if you are incorporated, you may receive one because your client isn't sure of your business' legal status. Double-check the amount shown on the 1099-Form to ensure accuracy because duplicates are given to the Federal government and they expect this income to show on your annual tax return.

Sometimes, people mistakenly record a loan to their business as income to the business—but it's not and you don't want to pay income taxes on the amount. Make sure that it's shown as a liability (debt) in your records. Also, if you invest money into the business it is not considered income. It's an equity investment (category #3 Equity). And, yes, all these categories will start to make sense as we see how they affect your reports. And, yes, we want reports so we know how your business is performing and how to make business decisions wisely!

Expenses

The fifth drawer (category #5) is for your operating expenses— those costs and expenses required to run your business (usually re-occurring costs). Keep file folders for the following records: rent, utilities, advertising, telephone, supplies, insurance, payroll, automobile, travel and any other expenses you may have. You should be keeping the following types of papers in these file folders: cash register purchase tapes, credit card sales slips, invoices from businesses where you purchased supplies, petty cash slips–any paper record of your transactions.

The purchase of an asset is not an expense and should be kept separate in the asset category. Even if you are allowed to 'expense' an asset for Federal income tax purposes, you'll probably want to keep it listed under assets (category #1). For example, a computer system is listed as an asset in your file folders and your reports. The IRS sometimes allows a business to write off the whole cost of the asset or a portion of the purchase each year as an 'expense' for the company. If the asset can be written off entirely during the year by your tax accountant, it's called a Section 179; whereas, if you 'expense' a portion of the asset each year, it's called a depreciation expense. See Chapter 9 for a discussion on depreciation.

Sometimes people record a payment on a loan as an expense– it is not. A check that is written to make a loan payment is often split into two parts: it's the repayment of the loan principal and its interest. Only the interest portion of the loan is an expense. You'll keep track of this amount in the expense category with a file folder named Interest Expense. The principal portion of these transactions will be kept in the liabilities drawer in the loan account. You can start seeing why business owners prefer computerized accounting systems.

Likewise, a withdrawal of cash from the business for the owner of the business is not considered an expense unless he/she is receiving a paycheck–then it is payroll expense. Remember, for the most part, sole proprietors don't receive paychecks, they'll receive withdrawals (draws) and you'll keep track of these in a withdrawal account.

BUSINESS DEDUCTIONS

Your business is allowed to deduct appropriate expenses in calculating your net income for Federal taxation purposes. These are usually defined as the costs of running your business. According to the IRS, "To be deductible, a business expense must be both ordinary and necessary. An ordinary expense is one that is common and accepted in your industry. A necessary expense is one that is helpful and appropriate for your trade or business. An expense does not have to be indispensable to be considered necessary."

Below is a partial list of business expenses that you'll want to consider as deductible:

- Phone service
- Internet service
- Dues and Publications
- Freight & Shipping
- Legal
- Insurance—liability, workman's comp, errors and omissions and health insurance
- Office supplies
- Advertising
- Marketing
- Collateral materials such as business cards, brochures, fliers, booklets, pens, coffee mugs, and other promotional items
- Utilities
- Repairs and maintenance of buildings and equipment
- Consulting services
- Accounting services
- Books and resource materials
- Continuing education, workshops and conferences related to your business
- Interest expense on loans and business accounts
- Bank Service Charges
- Postage

- Payroll for part-time, full-time and occasional employees
- Dues to organizations
- Donations
- Uniforms
- Property taxes
- Travel expenses such as airfare, parking fees, rental cars, hotels and meals
- Auto expenses: gas, repairs, licenses, insurance and maintenance OR you may wish to calculate your expenses based on mileage
- Rent and/or home office–If you are operating your business from a home office, there are many deductions for which you may be eligible. If you are in doubt about a specific deduction, create a separate account (file folder) and ask your accountant when your tax return is prepared. Basically, if you have a home business and you have a dedicated area in your home for running your business, you may be able to allocate a portion of your housing expenses to your business. There are strict guidelines for this and you'll wish to read the IRS Publication 587.

Summary of the Major Account Types

Up to now, we've been referring to your files as folders and the five cabinet drawers as categories. From now on, we're making a slight terminology shift and will be calling our file folders 'accounts' and the categories of the accounts, 'account types.' These accounts and major account types ultimately create your financial statements and reports in a manner consistent with Generally Accepted Accounting Principles (GAAP). GAAP provides a consistent system for accountants and business owners to follow so business records are standardized–making them easier to read and understand. The reports are a method of communicating the financial status of the company–a way of telling a story. If every accountant and every business owner created their own system, it would be difficult and time-consuming to understand the reports. The five major types of accounts are Assets, Liabilities, Equity, Income and Expenses.

Assets are everything that your business possesses–tangible and intangible–including checking accounts, savings accounts, inventory, A/R, furniture and equipment. Assets are usually broken into sub-groupings: current and fixed assets. Current assets are those that are short-term by nature, readily available to the business and are expected to be used or consumed within the year. Fixed assets are more permanent in nature and usually last longer than one year.

Liabilities are the debts that your business has acquired such as loans, credit cards and vender accounts. They are also broken into two primary components: current and long-term. Current liabilities are those that will be paid in less than one year. Long-term liabilities are those debts that take longer than one year to pay.

Equity accounts include the owner's investment and may be referred to as contributed capital. The bottom-line net profit from your business each year that you have not spent are retained and may be transferred to a special account with the name of Retained Earnings if you are using computerized software. The renaming of net profit to retained earnings happens on the last day of your fiscal year. Every business has a fiscal year, which is twelve months long and usually coordinates with a calendar year.

Income is the revenues your business has received from sales and services and **expenses** are the costs your business incurs for the purpose of earning that income.

By setting up your accounts and account types in a manner that is consistent and recognized by accountants and other industry professionals, you assist yourself in preparing reports that can be read and understood easily.

Next Chapter: Taking Charge—Tools for Cash Flow!

4

Taking Charge

Tools For Cash Flow

Now that your file folders provide a skeletal structure for your system, we'll talk about the process. These processes should be consistent and used daily so that they become ingrained and incorporated into your business. Eventually, they become second nature.

Let's Take the Money in!

Record a sales receipt–A sales receipt is usually used when payment is received at the time that goods and services are delivered to your customer or client. At the basic level, you can use a simple receipt book from an office supply store–or use one of the free templates downloadable from the Microsoft® website.

A sales receipt should include your business name and contact information, the customer's name and their contact information, customer number (when you're large enough to use them), the service and products that are being sold, the number of units being sold, the price for each, the total price, the inclusion of sales tax, the total amount that the customer is paying and a very bold thank you message.

By using a *sales receipt* (versus a *sales invoice*) you are indicating that the customer is paying when she receives the goods and services. You also include how the payment is made (cash, check or credit card). Make sure that you take the time to fill in the form immediately–do not depend on your memory to complete this form in the future.

Invoicing a customer–A *sales invoice* (versus a *sales receipt*) is prepared when you are providing credit (terms) to your clients and customers and the client's payment is due in the future. Your invoice form includes the same information that a sales receipt does, in addition to the specific credit terms. Using a form that is formatted differently from your sales receipts allows you to know at a glance if the client was invoiced and owes you money, or whether they paid at the time the goods and services were delivered. Make a small but definite distinction between these two forms and you will save yourself a lot of time and energy. When you invoice a customer, they owe you money and need to be added to your Accounts Receivable (A/R) list immediately.

Receive a payment–In the future, you'll receive payments from these invoiced clients. You'll want to mark 'paid' on your copies of their invoices and make a notation in your A/R list.

Make a deposit–When you receive checks from your clients, regardless of whether they are from sales receipts or from the payments for invoices, you'll want a special place to keep them until they are taken to the bank for deposit. Some people use a blue bank bag, the bottom desk drawer or a small office safe. It is not a good idea to allow the checks to pile up with unopened mail, file folders and other projects on your desk. It's easy to lose track of these checks and they need to be located in one place until deposited.

It is also important to deposit on a regular basis. That might be daily, three to four times a week or once a week. As you grow and have more checks with larger amounts of cash, make sure to deposit more frequently. Finding a bank with a night depository helps tremendously because it's convenient and you can drop off the deposits after-hours. A night depository is a special pull-out drawer that allows certain people access to drop deposits after hours. Access is controlled with the use of a key and you receive the key by asking the tellers for permission to use it.

Most banks also allow deposits to be made through an ATM machine at any time of the day or night. If your business has bulky deposits, be sure to ask your bank if the ATM can accept them. Many banks have recently started free courier services to pick-up your daily deposit. If your financial institution provides this service, take advantage of it and save yourself a trip! Another easy way to make deposits is by scanning them with a small scanner provided by your bank, or their app. For instance, I deposit checks by taking a picture on my smart phone and depositing digitally.

If you're forgetful or still need to make large physical deposits to banks, be sure that when you order your checks and deposit slips, order the deposit slips with duplicate copies. That way, if you're in a hurry, you can still make your deposit to the bank quickly. Use the deposit copy to make notes about the names of the clients for the checks that you are depositing. You can take the deposit to the bank and finish your transaction records later.

Conceptually, you'll record these transactions in your income accounts on your summary sheets in your file folders. Journals or notebooks can also be used to keep track of these different types of transactions. One of my clients keep a running tally of their sales, customer invoices and payments in two different notebooks (one for sales receipts, one for invoices). Just add your customer sales to the appropriate notebooks and create a running tally of the sales you've made and the customers you've invoiced. You will be able to know what your sales are at any time as well as which customers owe you money.

Ultimately, a computerized accounting system helps automate the workload, reducing your time commitment and potential errors from the transposing of numbers. Software will also ensure the accuracy of your monthly, quarterly and annual reports. The software cannot make a mathematical error.

Keep in mind, there is a learning curve with financial software. When you decide to implement one, you should continue using your manual system for a few months until you are confident using the new system. Eventually, all of your vendor and customer information needs to be transferred and the system should provide you with the reports and information you need quickly and easily.

Keeping track of your money coming from clients is important for your business. You'll know how much money you have and be able to budget wisely. Another reason to ensure your money-in system works well is to prevent annoying your clients with repeated reminders to pay when they've already paid. Your clients may think that you are unprofessional and question the use of your services in the future.

Monitoring and managing money coming in to your business can be one of the most satisfying aspects of your endeavor. It is rewarding to see money coming in from your hard work and efforts and providing you with a profit—confirmation that your business is performing well!

Money Out

The processes for spending your dollars should also be consistent and standardized. If and when you begin hiring employees, you will already have an easy-to-follow system in place and you'll feel confident that your methods are reliable.

Most people are basically honest and will stay honest when provided with guidelines that ensure that the checks-and-balances are in place. Checks-and-balances are a system that prevents one person from having total control of money transactions by having someone else check his or her work for accuracy. For instance, if one of your employees writes the checks, receives customers' payments, makes deposits and reconciles the bank statement, you or another trusted employee want to review that person's work. For further discussion on embezzlement protection see Chapter 8.

***Bills from vendors*–**You want a system for tracking the bills sent to you by vendors and suppliers. Leaving them in a pile on the floor, bookshelf or desk where you are unable to find them is not the best location. Letting your mail pile up in unopened envelopes is also not a recommended process.

Open your mail regularly–daily if possible, weekly at a minimum. When you receive bills, file them immediately into a special folder called 'Unpaid Bills'. The folder should hold nothing other than the bills, second reminders and letters attempting to collect the money due. You'll want to pay bills weekly or at least once every two to three weeks. When you make the payment, mark the date, how the payment was made (check number or credit or debit card) and the amount paid on the bill. Staple the bill together with any other notes regarding the bill and file it into its expense or asset file folder. Remember, not everything that a business purchases is an expense. Sometimes bills are for the purchase of an asset. When you file the bill in your file cabinet, enter the transaction onto the one page summary sheet located in the file folder.

Make sure that you record all your payments in your check register–that's the little book that comes with your checks. It is used for keeping a running total of your bank deposits, your checks and your balance in the bank. Your computer software also has a check register. Keeping this information helps you with your bank reconciliation (to be discussed later in this chapter).

Some people like to use an additional file folder named 'Filing' or 'To Be Filed.' They allocate special time for the filing process when the folder is full. Personally, I like to pay my bills, record them and file at the same time. It removes the clutter from the

office and at the same time it removes one more chore from the list of all the things you have to do. You'll want to try to stay on the same schedule weekly to form a good habit.

It is important to pay bills regularly (at least monthly). Waiting until your vendors call to remind you that a payment is due will not improve the relationship or your credit history. If you don't have enough money to pay all the bills, it is important to make partial payments to each vendor. When you are having a cash flow problem it is not only polite but also imperative to your business that you contact each vendor by phone to let him or her know that you'll send a partial payment in good faith. Also, let them know when you will send an additional payment.

Making a phone call shows that you take the issue seriously and it's more thoughtful than jotting a quick e-mail. Show them the courtesy that you want others to show you when they are having difficulties. A confirmation e-mail can document your intentions and conversation in writing. Make good on your promises.

Furthermore, if you are unable to afford an item, don't buy it with the expectation that another business will carry your debt for you. If you really need the item, there are many ways to acquire it with a creative solution—work out a barter, create a lay-away plan or rent the item instead of purchasing it. Talk to the supplier and see what she can do to help you be creative. You'll be pleasantly surprised.

Bank Reconciliations

There are a number of reasons you should reconcile your bank accounts monthly. Reconciliation is a term to describe the process of comparing your records with the bank records and ensuring both your business records and the bank's records are accurate.

When you spend money from your checking or savings accounts, you need to know how much money is left in the account. In the past, it was easy to forget to record a check. Now, it is even easier to forget to record ATM withdrawals, automatic

Electronic Funds Transfers (EFT), debit card purchases and online bill payments.

A monthly reconciliation ensures that you don't continue writing checks and making purchases when money is not available in the account. If you have over-draft protection on your account, those purchases won't 'bounce' but they may cost you lots of money. My bank charges $25 for each day of overdraft. Some banks send an email immediately when an overdraft has occurred. Unfortunately for me, my bank sends an Insufficient Funds notice in the mail, which takes at least eight days to arrive. I can think of plenty of things to do with $200, other than pay bank fees. I use online banking services almost entirely and check my balances in every account at least weekly to make sure that the previous mentioned nightmare doesn't happen.

In addition to our own errors, forgetfulness, and lack of interest, and in spite of computerized systems, banks continue to make mistakes. Tellers transpose (reverse) numbers, deposits are entered into incorrect accounts and transfers are made that whisk your money elsewhere. At the extreme, bank employees may embezzle funds from customers that they suspect are not paying attention to their own accounts. The news media reports on these episodes regularly. I am familiar with two incidents in our local area.

If you have a bookkeeper or employee reconcile your monthly bank statements, I strongly recommend that you examine the reconciliation report and ask several questions. With some simple questions you may prevent embezzlement by employees that are helping you with your accounting.

In addition to reconciling checking and savings accounts, you should also reconcile credit card accounts and loan accounts. By starting immediately with a new account you'll understand the process and the task will become easy, even as your statements become more complicated.

Clients that have never reconciled always as, "How far back should I start?" The answer is, "It depends." If we're talking years, I certainly wouldn't go back to the first month and reconcile a gazillion months, one by one, unless I was building a case for embezzlement, suspecting missing funds, looking for major mistakes or needing completely accurate records from the start date. This is always a difficult decision because if you don't start at the beginning you will need to make adjustments to your records to force them to balance—these adjustments are called journal entries. If your tax returns have been completed for a number of years, you will want to obtain your accountant's advice prior to adjusting previous years' records. If you start adjusting previous years' records, you may have to file new adjusted tax returns.

Let's say that you haven't reconciled for this year. I would begin with the first month of the year and move forward. Keep in mind that if you begin with this month's statement you can reconcile previous months as well—but only in a manual system. If you're using a computerized accounting system, you cannot work 'backwards'—you must start with the earliest month that you ultimately want reconciled and reconcile forward.

WALKING THROUGH A BANK RECONCILIATION

I tease my clients that the secret to performing a perfect bank reconciliation is simple … don't write any checks and never make any deposits! Obviously, unrealistic!

In performing reconciliations, you'll want your bank balance (check register) to match the balance that the bank shows on the monthly statement. This rarely happens because there are transactions that your business has made that haven't quite reached the bank, and there are transactions the bank made that you may have forgotten to record in your business records. The reconciliation process basically asks the question, "**When** all checks and deposits clear the bank, will the two balances match?"

Most bank statements received monthly are broken into sections: one for deposits and another for checks, and they are usually listed in the order that the transaction cleared the bank.

Your bank may have a mid-month cut-off date. Ask them if this can be changed to reflect a bank statement that shows transactions monthly. Not all bank statements are formatted in an easy-to-read manner and credit unions usually have statements that show all transactions chronologically regardless of whether the transaction is a deposit or withdrawal. This makes reconciling a little more difficult but still manageable.

To get started, make a copy of your bank statement. You'll be making tic marks and notes on the copy and it is nice to preserve the original statement free of these notes, figures and erasures. Begin by comparing the bank statement to your check register.

Use a pencil to make a tic mark, such as a "/" or "✓", on both the bank statement copy and in your check register when you locate a matching transaction on each. Because they tend to be chronological, this part of the process is relatively easy. Once complete, you may have transactions that have cleared your bank account that are not listed in your check register. Enter these immediately into your register and place a mark next to them and also on the statement copy. Recalculate your ending balance in your check register. Through the process of elimination, you are left with very few entries to ponder.

You may also have transactions that are in your checking account register but not shown on your bank account statement– they have not yet cleared your bank. This happens when checks and other transactions have been entered into your business checking register close to the end of the month and the bank hasn't paid them yet. Or, for some reason the vendor hasn't cashed or deposited the check yet. The uncleared transactions are called outstanding and sometimes can be outstanding or pending for quite a while.

Below are two examples of basic bank reconciliations:

EXAMPLE 1

Bank Balance from your Bank Statement	$ 9,000.00
Add the Deposits that have not cleared your bank	
	$ 0.00
	$
Subtract the Checks that have not cleared your bank	
Outstanding checks	-$22.13
Outstanding checks	-$187.93
Outstanding checks	-$211.14
Outstanding checks	-$79.58
Outstanding checks	-$49.09
This total should match your check register	$8,450.13

Summary of Reconciliation

Balance on Bank Statement:	$9,000.00
Balance in business' check register:	$8,450.13
Difference between the two balances:	$ 549.87
Outstanding checks not cleared yet:	$ 549.87

When the outstanding checks clear the bank, the balance on the bank statement is the same as the one on my check register–$8,450.13 ... hooray! You're in balance!

EXAMPLE 2

Bank Balance from your Bank Statement	$9,000.00
Add the Deposits that have not cleared your bank	
	$
	$
Subtract the Checks that have not cleared your bank	
Outstanding checks	-$112.87
Outstanding checks	-$96.34
Outstanding checks	-$290.79
Outstanding checks	$
Outstanding checks	$
This total should match your check register	$8,500.00

Summary of Reconciliation

Balance on Bank Statement:	$9,000.00
Balance in business' check register:	$8,450.13
Difference between the two balances:	$ 549.87
Outstanding checks not cleared yet:	$ 500.00

When the $500 in outstanding transactions clear the bank, the bank's new statement balance will be $8,500.00. Oops … not in balance yet. Compared to our balance of $8,450.13, the bank indicates that we have more money in our bank account than we think we have. Our account is 'off' by $49.87. So we are either missing a deposit for the amount or we are not including an outstanding check in our outstanding checks computation. We should locate the missing transactions.

This process becomes more difficult when there are multiple transactions that have not been recorded in the register and multiple transpositions of numbers. A transposition is when you switch the numbers. For instance, instead of $511.21, you have recorded $115.12. Transposed numbers are always difficult to find because our eyes visually recognize them as the same number. There is a mathematical 'Rule of 9' for transposed numbers that sometimes helps. Take the number that you are 'off' and if you can divide it by '9' evenly, then you have a transposition. However, this only works when there is one mistake, not multiple ones. If you are having difficulty, it may help to have another person look at your reconciliation with fresh eyes.

There is no magic wand. Each transaction that has not cleared the bank needs to be accounted for. If you know that a check was just sent, that's fine. Of course, the use of a computerized accounting system simplifies this process and is a great time saver. However, many of the difficulties can be minimized even in a manual system if withdrawals and deposits are entered into the checking registers carefully, correctly and on a regular basis. The small steps of being careful and deliberate save you time, effort and tears later.

This basic bank reconciliation may be downloaded as a spreadsheet for **Free** from www.marie-gibson.com.

Example of Basic Bank Reconciliation	
Bank Balance from your Bank Statement	$
Add the Deposits that have not cleared your bank	
	$
	$
	$
Subtract the Checks that have not cleared your bank	
Outstanding checks	$
Outstanding checks	$
Outstanding checks	$
Outstanding checks	$
Subtotal	$
This total should match your check register	$

You may also need to watch for transactions that are not recorded in your check register but are shown on your bank statement, such as interest earned, service fees and forgotten transactions. Record these transactions in your check register and re-adjust the balance.

Daily Batch and Reconciliation for Your Cash Drawer

For retail businesses, restaurants and others that maintain a cash register, a daily reconciliation (batch) of your cash drawer is imperative, especially if you have employees. The reconciliation form shows how much cash your business started with at the beginning of the day, what sales you made, whether the sales were cash, check or credit card, if there were any refunds or small purchases (using money from the register) and, ultimately, how much cash you have at the end of the day.

If your business uses a cash register and you accept cash, checks and credit cards, then you'll want to reconcile the cash register every day. This process should be simple and easy to understand by your employees so that it's done accurately. Some businesses provide for full batch reconciliations between shifts. Each employee is responsible for balancing their own cash drawer.

Most cash registers will produce reports at the day's end (or at shift's end) that are printed on the cash register tape. Sometimes they are called 'X' reports and 'Z' reports. Usually an 'X' report can be taken at any time of the day and as many times as desired. It provides an ongoing summary of sales and other details. The 'Z' report is taken at the end of the day, only once, and it zeroes out the cash register information for the day. The next day (or the next shift), the information starts again.

The batch report will provide you information about your sales, sales tax and your bank deposits. You should be able to prepare your bank deposits (cash, checks and credit cards) from this information, and you should be able to know exactly what your sales revenue was and your taxable amount due to the state. You may also wish to have your sales broken into departments so that you can track what merchandise sells the fastest.

Shown below you will see a basic daily batch report for a single register where an owner is tracking sales from different departments.

- Record the sales, sales tax and gross receipts.
- Count and record your ending cash. Most businesses leave the same amount of money in the cash register to start the next day. Subtract it and return the amount to the drawer.
- Subtract any refunds and purchases that were made

during the day and your total will be the amount of money that is expected to be in the drawer.

- ◆ Create your bank deposit by recording what money is being sent to the bank. Often times, you will automatically send your credit card information to the bank separately but it still needs to be included here to balance.

- ◆ When you have your total funds going to the bank, compare it with the total monies that are expected to be in the drawer.

- ◆ You may be over or short, and will need to determine if it's enough to investigate. Each business will set its own policy regarding an 'acceptable' level of over/shorts for a day.

- ◆ Be sure to include general information regarding the day of the week, the employee's name, etc. This is great information to have if you decide to track sales patterns.

Basic Daily Batch Report	
Sales Dept 1 _____	Deposit to Bank
+ Sales Dept 2 _____	Cash _____
+ Sales Dept 3 _____	+ Checks _____
+ Sales Dept 4 _____	+ Credit Cards _____
= Total Sales _____	= Total Funds to Bank _____
+ Sales Tax _____	- Total Monies Expected _____
= Gross Receipts $ _____	= Over/Short $_____
Gross Receipts $ _____	Name _____
+ Beginning Cash _____	Date _____
- Refunds _____	Day of the Week _____
- Purchases _____	Comments _____
= Total Monies Expected $____	

It is important to have a system. Even a simple system helps you track your money and have good, accurate reports that you can use for making smart decisions. Be sure to use a money-in system and money-out system, reconcile your bank accounts monthly and learn how to protect yourself and your money from your employees and contractors. In the next chapter, you're going to learn how your basic system feeds directly into those reports, how the reports are created and how interrelated they are with your system and your records.

Next Chapter: Financial Reports—How *To Create Good Ones*

5

Financial Reports

How to Create Good Ones

In this chapter, we examine how your accounts are summarized and flow into your reports. You were originally asked to envision your file folders (accounts) in specific drawers and these five specific groups became your five types of accounts: assets, liabilities, net worth, income, and expenses. Even if you don't physically file in five drawers, you want to maintain the image or the perspective of these five distinct types of accounts. Each type of account is interrelated in your financial statements, thus flowing to your reports in a specific manner. It is important to create these financial statements at least monthly, if not more frequently. As a business owner, you'll want the dynamic feedback that they provide about your income, costs and cash flows on a regular basis. This storytelling process is an imperative part of being a business owner.

Summarizing the bottom two drawers (accounts) of your file cabinet provides you with a total of your income and your expenses. You can create an Income Statement (sometimes called the Profit and Loss or P&L report) from this information by subtracting your expenses from your income. This report is the easiest to read because it is so similar to your personal budget. And, exactly like your personal budget, you sometimes have more expenses than income. The proper terms for the bottom line of this report are Net Income or Net Loss, sometimes referred to as your Net Profit. It's the profit left over after paying expenses, or the loss you incurred during a particular time period. An income statement (P&L or Profit and Loss report) is always created for a period of time—a week, a month, a quarter, a year or other specific time period. We say "the net income for the month of January is $____ or the net loss for the second quarter is $___."

One of the hardest concepts to remember is that not all of the money that businesses spend is for expenses. Some of the cash pays for assets and some payments may be for loans. Loan payments have to be split into two accounts: one for the principal portion that's applied toward the repayment of the debt, and one for the interest payments. Principal payments are recorded against the original loan (a liability); interest payments are recorded as expenses—specifically in an interest expense account. You probably need only one account for all your interest expense.

Likewise, not all of the purchases of assets and payments of expenses are paid with cash; sometimes we use loans and credit cards, thus increasing our liabilities. This is a reminder that you should have and use the summary sheets in your accounts (file folders) to record (post) an entry to keep your balances correct.

It is the process of making a distinction with the smaller details that determines whether your reports appear correctly. Remember, if you have accidentally filed an asset as an expense, you simply move it from that expense category to the asset category. And, many of your assets eventually become expenses through a process of obsolescence or depreciation.

Your assets have a specific life expectancy and their values need to be written off a little bit every year as an expense (this is called depreciation). Your accountant and tax advisor need to know the assets you purchase each year to help you gain the advantage of using these costs as tax expense deductions. He or she will ask you specifically about the purchase of assets to determine if they can be written off immediately (for tax purposes), or if they must be depreciated over a period of years. As these assets are written off and become expenses, the correct amount is transferred from the asset category to the expense category. These transfers of value from an asset to an expense are done entirely with journal entries and are non-cash expenses. Depreciation expense is shown in your income statement, whereas Accumulated Depreciation is the account used to reduce the value of your asset in your balance sheet. We discuss depreciation more in Chapter 9.

Because your 'cash-out' can be used for different purposes (expenses and assets) and your 'cash-in' comes from different sources, and you have non-cash expenses that need to be recorded properly, it is imperative to become familiar with the accounts that are recorded on the income statement and with those that are recorded on the balance sheet.

Simple Income Statement

If you are not using financial software, you are still able to create financial reports each month by using a spreadsheet (as shown below) that helps you organize your subtotals. A simple income statement should be reviewed monthly, at a minimum. It should reflect the expenses that your business acquired in the effort of creating the corresponding income. The concept of recording the expenses that are associated with your income for each time period is called 'matching' and is an important concept in accounting. In addition to the income and expense dollars, it's very helpful to show your income and expenses as a percentage of the total. An income statement expressed in dollars alone does not always encourage you to question the numbers. However, a percentage that is extraordinarily high or changes dramatically from one month to the next is easily observed.

While your business is small, you may only look at this report monthly, but as your business grows, you will find yourself looking at this more frequently. It provides you feedback as to how well your company is doing and if you are making a profit. When reviewing this report, be sure to observe if you have unusually high expenses that prohibited your business from earning a profit. Sometimes, we sell our goods and services at a rate that doesn't allow for a profit and we only realize this when we see it in a written format. Many business owners know exactly the source and amount of income, but they don't always realize the source and amount of expenses related in acquiring it. The income statement makes sure an owner associates expenses to the income earned to see how the business is performing. In other words, what expenses did it take you to earn the income? This is an important concept for you to grasp conceptually and is called accrual basis accounting (see Chapter 9 for further discussion).

By making regular use of your income statement, you will learn why and when your business earns a profit and what expenses prohibit you from doing so. The more you evaluate this report, the more you will like it.

Find a **FREE**, downloadable copy of an income statement template at **http://mariegibson.com/IncomeStatementSpreadsheet.html**

	Jan	%	Feb	%	March	%
Sales and Revenues						
Hourly Consulting						
Workshop Training						
Custom Projects						
E-books						
Retail Sales						
Interest Income						
Total Income						
Expenses						
Rent						
Telephone						
Office Supplies						
Insurance						
Promos & Advertising						
Travel						
Meals						
Entertainment						
Automobile						
Airfare						
Hotel						
Depreciation Expense						
Bank Service Fees						
Total Expenses						
NET INCOME (LOSS)						

Balance Sheet

Many business owners understand income statements quickly because they are similar to personal budgets–basically, income and expenses. However, it is equally important to examine and understand another report–your balance sheet. The balance sheet accounts are intricately connected with the transactions that affect your Profit and Loss report. Yet, sometimes business owners neglect to read and understand the changes in it. A balance sheet shows the financial position of a business at a specific given point in time–*on a specific date.* Remember, the income statement is shown *for a period of time.* Your balance sheet shows your checking and savings account balances, other assets such as inventory and A/R (Accounts Receivable) as well as liabilities that the business might have acquired to purchase the assets or pay expenses. Simply put, your balance sheet shows the relationship between your assets, your liabilities and your equity on one specific day.

If you took each of the top three drawers (types of accounts) of our imaginary file cabinet (assets, liabilities, and equity) and summarized them into one report, it is called a balance sheet. The report details what the business owns (assets), its level of debts (liabilities) and net worth or equity on a specific day.

Most business owners have vague ideas about what a balance sheet does and how to interpret the information provided on one. My clients seem to have three primary ideas and understandings of a balance sheet, so I'm going to use each of the three perspectives to explain the concepts more fully.

PERSPECTIVE ONE OF UNDERSTANDING BALANCE SHEETS: WHAT IS **NET WORTH?**

In its simplest form, a balance sheet reflects the *relationship* between your accounts. The balance sheet shows you what the relationship, or difference is, between your assets and your liabilities. This difference is your equity or net worth. It is always organized and expressed as this:

$$\begin{array}{rl} & \text{Assets} \\ \text{minus} & < \text{Liabilities} \\ \hline \text{equals} & = \text{Equity (Net worth)} \end{array}$$

You'll want to watch the net worth or the value of your business grow each year, and you'll want to learn how the balance sheet reflects this value. Net worth may be comprised of three components: Personal investment funds, partner or shareholder investment funds and Retained Earnings. Retained earnings is the running accumulation of net profit that the business earns each year and is left in the business to grow and expand.

A personal example that many people understand is the value of your home. For instance, if you bought a house for $120,000 and your mortgage debt is $100,000, your equity in the home is $20,000. This is its 'book' value of your equity; its true value depends on the market.

A simple business example–If you had to close your business today and liquidate your assets, you would have to then pay off the loans or debts associated with acquiring those assets. For instance, if you sell your business for $100,000 and have no debt, the net worth is $100,000 and you, the business owner, keep $100,000.

Or, if you sell the assets for $100,000 and pay off loans of $60,000, the net worth of the business is $40,000. This is the excess of the assets after paying the business debts (the net worth)–this is different thanearned profit, this is the equity of your business.

Goodwill–Keep in mind that businesses, just like houses, are often sold for more or less than their net worth depending on economic factors, negotiation abilities, potential for additional revenues, outstanding liabilities and emotional reasons. Businesses that are run by a sole proprietor may be difficult to sell because without the owner's knowledge and expertise, the value of the business is questionable. When a business is sold for more than its net worth, the term is called Goodwill and is usually associated with a strong business presence, solid client base and other market advantages. Goodwill is listed on the new owner's balance sheet as an Other Asset, and is amortized over several years. Amortization is similar to depreciation—it is the term that is used for the devaluation and expensing of non-tangible items like patents, copyrights, trademarks, and goodwill.

PERSPECTIVE TWO OF UNDERSTANDING BALANCE SHEETS: WHAT'S YOUR BUSINESS WORTH?

Another way of looking at the information on a balance sheet is to recognize that it expresses a *value* of the business. By adding all your assets and subtracting all your liabilities (debts), you are showing what your business is worth—its equity.

The balance sheet presents the 'book value' of your assets by showing the original amount paid for the assets minus their depreciation. As the assets age, they are worth less, so their values are decreased—they are depreciated. The IRS allows many types of depreciation for tax purposes (these different types are discussed further in Chapter 9). Once the annual depreciation amount is determined, you want to reflect it properly on your balance sheet. For instance, if you are depreciating your furniture, you show the original cost of the furniture as an asset and the depreciation for the furniture in a contra account—meaning that the depreciation is subtracted from the original cost.

The current or 'book' value of the asset is its original purchase price minus the amount of accumulated depreciation and is shown on your balance sheet as:

	Furniture	$ 35,000
minus <	Accumulated Depreciation	-15,000
equals =	Furniture, Net:	$20,000

The book value of your liabilities is the original amount of debt adjusted by your accumulated principal payments. Be sure not to subtract your interest expense from the balance of the loan.

PERSPECTIVE THREE OF UNDERSTANDING
BALANCE SHEETS

We've been looking at different ways of understanding our balance sheets and we started with the accounting formula:

$$Assets - Liabilities = Net\ Worth\ (Equity)$$

Now we're going to shift it a little bit and examine the statement using the same formula written in a different way:

$$Assets = Liabilities + Net\ Worth\ (Equity)$$

Let's start by assuming that a business owns a certain amount of financial assets, for instance $10,000. The business *acquired* those *assets from one of two places.* Either:

♦ through the acquisition of liabilities (taking out a loan to purchase the assets) or

♦ through the use of the owner's or partners' investment (capital).

Therefore, the assets **MUST** equal the total of the investment and the debt combined. For instance, if the business has debt of $2,000 (assets still being $10,000), we know that the owner(s) invested $8,000 in the business to acquire the remaining assets. Or, if the business has debt of $9,000 (assets remaining at $10,000), the owner only invested $1,000 in the business. If your assets are worth $10,000 with no debt, the value or equity investment of your business is $10,000.

A business with a lot of debt does not possess a solid foundation. A potential financial lender wishes to see a strong equity position when lending money to a business. While underwriting loans for a micro-lending organization, prospective business owners often wish to invest $1,000 to $2,000 of their own money and will ask to borrow $35,000 from the lender. Even for micro-lenders that's extremely high risk and seldom will a lender feel comfortable making such a loan.

We've approached the income statement and the balance sheet from different perspectives and now have a basic understanding of these two simple reports. The income statement and the balance sheet are interrelated and changes in one make changes in the other. For instance, your cash balance is shown on the balance sheet and is directly affected by the receiving of money and payment of funds from customers and clients. Furthermore, if your business has Accounts Payables and Accounts Receivables, these are summarized on the balance sheet, and again, changes to these two accounts result from adjustments in your income and your purchases (both expenses and assets). There is another account that directly links your income statement and your balance sheet resulting in frequent changes between the accounts that are summarized on the two reports, and that is your cost of goods sold.

COST OF GOODS (SERVICES) SOLD

For businesses with retail or wholesale sales, merchandise (inventory) is purchased and then resold. The accounting for tracking this inventory movement is not a one-step process like the tracking of other operating and overhead expenses. In order for your reports to be accurate, these costs must be classified correctly *as they flow into* your warehouse or storeroom and then *as they move out* of the warehouse or storeroom to your customers through sales. Tracking the process of inventory slightly changes the basic format of your simple income statement.

When merchandise inventory is purchased it is recorded as a Current Asset (assets that have a life-span of less than one year) at the cost you pay for it (the wholesale cost). The inventory remains in the assets account until it is sold, at which time its value is moved into a Cost of Goods Sold (COGS) account. COGS (as it is normally called) should reflect the cost that you paid for the item and any additional alterations once you've received it. In more sophisticated accounting systems, specifically manufacturing job costing systems and some service businesses, COGS consist of a number of factors, sometimes including payroll and some proportion of overhead.

Once your business sales reach a certain level, it is difficult to constantly track the COGS each time an item is sold and many businesses shift to computerized systems or Point of Sale software or they estimate this adjustment amount each month. For instance, if you normally purchase items for $10 and sell them for $20, when your monthly sales reach $2,000 your estimated COGS is $1,000. In other words, your monthly income of $2,000 is achieved by selling the inventory that had a direct cost of goods sold of $1,000.

When the value of inventory available for sale is recorded as an asset and summarized it shows on the balance sheet as Inventory. However, the COGS account is summarized and shown on your income statement (P&L) just below the revenues. The difference found by subtracting the COGS from Sales Revenues is known as the Gross Profit. After the COGS is subtracted from the Revenues, then you subtract your other operating expenses from the Gross Profit to find your net income or loss. For instance, it would appear to be:

	Sales Revenue (Income)
minus	< COGS (Cost of Goods Sold)
equals	= Gross Profit
minus	< Operating Expenses
equals	= Net Income (loss)

As the number of sales transactions grow, the transferring of inventory assets to the COGS account becomes important in the resulting net income. If your COGS is too low, then your net income is overstated and you will pay too much tax on the net income. If your COGS is too high, then your net income appears low and you pay too few taxes. To determine accurate COGS, many businesses take an end-of-year inventory count of their items to calculate their COGS. This is a relatively simple formula and it is always calculated at your cost for the goods.

	Beginning Inventory Value[1]
plus	+ Inventory purchases during the year
equals	= Value of inventory available to sell to customers
minus	< Ending inventory value[2]
equals	= COGS (value of what you actually did sell at wholesale cost)

1. The beginning Inventory value is on the first day of your fiscal year.

2. The ending inventory value is on the last day of your fiscal year.

Simple Statement of Cash Flow

Statement of Cash Flows is a report that shows how your accounts are affected by the movement of your cash coming in and going out of the business. It is primarily used to determine if the business has enough money to pay its bills and other obligations when they become due.

A Statement of Cash Flows and the income statement are often not the same because your income statement shows the income when it's earned (not collected) and your expenses when they occur (not when you pay them). This is called accrual basis accounting (a discussion of accrual basis accounting can be found in Chapter 9).

In one month you may have a million dollars of sales recorded on your income statement, and yet receive no payments from clients. In turn, you will not be able to pay your expenses, purchase assets and pay your loans. A statement of cash flows records cash coming into the business not just from your client payments, but also from the borrowing of funds and other investments. Furthermore, the cash going out of your business will include those not just for expenses, but purchase of assets, inventory and payments of loans.

There are a couple of ways to create a cash flow statement and

I present one of the simplest ones here. It will look similar to your income statement, but remember, its sole purpose is to recognize *cash movement* to make sure you have enough money to fulfill your obligations and to keep your business thriving.

Beginning Cash Balance	$
Cash In	
Cash Sales	
Payments from A/R clients	
Proceeds from new loans	
Sale of your assets	
Cash Out	
Payment of operating expenses	
Payments for inventory	
Cash purchase of new assets	
Payments of loans	
Withdrawals by owners, partners or shareholders	
Net Cash flow	$
Ending Cash Balance	$

As we've seen, each type of account flows to your three major reports in a very specific manner so that it becomes standardized in a way that business professionals can read and understand. Be sure to use the five types of accounts to organize your system and watch how your financial statements become an asset to you.

Next Chapter: Your Newest, Best Friend!

6

Your Newest, Best Friend

Interviewing and Hiring Accountants

Accounting professionals come in all shapes and sizes and are an important part of your business because they can provide an extraordinary range of services. He or she should be your newest, best friend. These educated professionals can provide a continuing wealth of information for all business owners. They are required to take classes regularly to remain current on new laws and issues that affect accounting and business tax returns. In this chapter, I discuss how to interview accountants, what type of questions to ask, what to expect and how to interact with them.

Ask people you know and trust if they use an accountant they respect and are willing to refer. If you are new to a community, become involved with the business networking organizations and be sure to ask for referrals. Plan to visit two or three accountants that have been recommended by other business colleagues prior to selecting one.

There are different types of accountants and accountants can offer several types of services depending on your needs. Certified Public Accountants (CPA's) are known primarily for preparing tax returns and reviewing and auditing corporate, business and

non-profit organization records. Managerial Accountants, certified through the Institute of Management Accountants (IMA), help you make sound management decisions based on the analysis of your financial records and other internal reports.

CPA's are licensed through a state exam and each state has a website with their current CPA licensees listed. It provides the office address, license number, original license date, expected expiration date and the current status of the accountant. If you are planning to hire a CPA, double-check this website to ensure that the accountant is currently licensed.

Some accountants will meet with you for an initial, complimentary hour, while others charge a minimal fee. This does not reflect on their ability, it is just a difference in operating policies. Be sure to ask what their initial consultation fee is when you call to schedule an appointment. Let each accountant know that you are interested in creating an ongoing working relationship with them to effectively manage your business' finances. An accountant can advise you on a regular schedule (weekly, monthly, quarterly), instead of 'just doing your annual tax return.' The money you spend receiving guidance during the year is more than offset by the benefits you receive, including a lower rate on your final tax return. 'Guidance' money is money well spent.

When you are visiting your accountant for the first time, have a number of questions ready. For instance, you'll want to know whether the majority of his business is working with small, entrepreneurial businesses or larger corporations. If you are in a specialized industry, you'll want an accountant that has background, experience and expertise in that area. Ask if you will be required to use his or her particular computerized software and how the work is going to be performed. Will you be providing records on a regular basis or is there a staff member that can help you with your monthly records? Is the staff member willing to provide feedback and help you and your employees learn to improve your records?

How will the logistics work? Some accountants use a delivery service to pickup documents, while others use remote access capabilities via the Internet. Is there a junior staff member assigned to your business? How often is the work of that person examined by the senior accountant? You'll also want to ask about the fee structure. Each member of an accountant's office may be billed at different rates or you may be billed a flat rate. It's important to ask.

Prepare your questions beforehand and conduct the interview in a professional manner. Do not overstay your welcome, usually one hour is plenty of time to discuss your business and ask questions about the prospective relationship. At the end of the visit, be sure to thank the accountant for his or her time and interest. If you have received a complimentary visit write a thank-you note within a few days. It may sound old-fashioned, yet good manners and courtesy are always appreciated. Let each accountant know as soon as possible if you would like to work with him or her, or if you opt for other professional representation. In the future, you may decide that you would like to work with one of the accountants you didn't initially select. Building a good relationship from the onset is important. Furthermore, if they know that you are a grateful and an appreciative business owner, they will refer customers to you.

It is also important to feel the information you have shared is confidential, that the accountant has a high level of integrity. If you hear the accountant or staff discussing another business in your presence, in a manner that is identifiable, you should look elsewhere.

Furthermore, there are accountants with as many different financial philosophies as there are business owners. You and your accountant should fundamentally agree on your level of risk aversion. It is important to discuss this in advance with your accountant.

Ultimately, it is important to select an accountant with good listening skills whom you can trust and one with empathy towards teaching you, correcting your mistakes and guiding you as you learn to create your accounting system. Select an accountant that can become your long-term advisor.

Working with Your Accountant

When you begin working with a new accountant, you'll want to share your chart of accounts with him or her. This list shows the accountant how you have organized your accounts and what your reports will look like. However, your accountant may prefer to provide you with his or her standard chart of accounts. He isn't implying that the one you've created is incorrect; he's just trying to make his life easier, thus saving you money.

If all of an accountant's clients use the same chart of accounts it makes it easier for the staff members. Ask the accountant to compare the two listings with you so that you understand the distinctions between them. If the two listings are relatively the same, it's easy to convert your system. If not, discuss the proposed changes. If the accountant responds defensively, you may wish to re-evaluate the relationship.

The accountant's chart of accounts may also have additional accounts that you don't have or need. You may wish to start using them or just delete them. After a while, you may find that a recommended account helps you with your accounting records and you'll add it into your files and your records. Be open to the fact that the accounts and system that you start with during your first year will look different than the system and accounts that you have in five years.

Once you begin working with the accountant, you want to meet at least quarterly to discuss the direction and volume of your business and to ask any questions regarding your accounting records. Accountants are used to dealing with business owners that are in the process of learning. Take notes and review them when you return to the office. It's easier to learn accounting if you have smaller, regular meetings with your accountant than one, large session annually. Avoid saving all your questions until the end of the year. Accounting offices are tightly scheduled from January through mid-April and you will receive better service at other times of the year.

At the end of the year, have your records organized for your accountant to review. Take the extra time to organize your files, your accounts and records and be sure to summarize your pages inside the file folders. Create a simple income statement and a balance sheet. If you pay the accountant to provide this service, it is very expensive. You or your employee can easily take care of this yourself.

Your accountant can provide different levels of service for your business. Keep in mind that the more you can organize for your own business, the more your accountant can concentrate on advising you.

Common Accounting Terminology

Learning commonly used terminology is important in any industry. Correctly using the words will help you feel more confident. You may already be familiar with many of these terms; however, I wanted to provide a basic list for people that are just beginning to learn the language. There are rules for any game that you play, so consider that you are learning the rules/terminology of a new game.

The following terms will allow you to converse with your accountant professionally:

- ◆ **Generally Accepted Accounting Principles** (GAAP). – The standards and issues statements accountants must adhere to (these are created by a governing body).
- ◆ **Chart of Accounts** – List of your 'file folders' (accounts) that organize your records.
- ◆ **Account** – one of your 'file folders.'
- ◆ **Bank Statement** – a report from your bank telling you about your banking activity during the month.
- ◆ **Bank Reconciliation** – comparing the bank's statement

ACCOUNTING 1, 2, 3 FOR BUSY BUSINESS OWNERS

with your records to make sure that they match. Mistakes can happen on either part.

- **Budget** – a plan on how you are going to spend money and earn money in your business.
- **Accounts Payable** – a list of money you owe to vendors and suppliers.
- **Accounts Receivable** – a list of money your customers and clients owe to you.
- **Inventory** – items you purchase with the intent of reselling; or materials that you use to create items to sell.
- **Income, Sales Revenues, Gross Income** – sales from items and services.
- **Expenses** – expenses related to operating your business.
- **Sales Taxes** – state taxes that you collect from your customers when they purchase from you. Your business is required to collect these taxes and remit them to the state, either monthly or quarterly on special forms provided by the state. Only a few states are sales tax exempt (see the discussion on sales tax in Chapter 7 for more information).
- **Invoice** – a form (or letter) that you give to your clients that shows the work you performed or the items they purchased, and when payment is due.
- **Independent Contractor** – a contractor who performs work for others and is not an employee.
- **Financial Statements** – reports that summarize, communicate and tell a story about your business' performance to yourself and others.
- **Income statement, Profit and Loss Report** (P&L) – a summary of income and expenses for a specific period of time i.e.; a month, quarter or year.
- **Net Profit, Net Loss** – by subtracting your expenses from your income, your business has either a profit or a loss.

- **Assets** – all items, tangible and intangible that your business owns.
- **Liabilities** – all debts that your business owes to others.
- **Owner's Investment Capital** – the amount of money (funds) and/or equipment that you give to the business to start.
- **Balance sheet** – a report that summarizes your assets and how your business funded them, either by debt (liabilities) or by owner's equity investment.
- **Cash Flow Statement** – will help you visualize the amount and the timing of your cash coming in and going out.

This basic terminology may feel a little awkward at times, but remember, if you aren't comfortable, it's because you are learning to speak a new language–the language of business.

Reports You Need to Prepare for the Accountant at Year's End

Many small business owners keep their own records or have a bookkeeper help them with their accounting throughout the year, and prefer to have an accountant prepare their income tax returns at the end of the year.

In order for your return to be accurately prepared, you want to provide the following information and reports to your accountant:

- Summary Profit and loss
- Detailed Profit and loss
- Balance sheet (a simple one's fine)
- A list of assets your business bought and sold during the year
- A list of the debts your business incurred and paid throughout the year including those made to the business by the owner.
- Documents showing any equity investment and/or draws

that the owner made to or from the business.

- Your Federal tax number
- Your sales tax records and copies of sales tax reports submitted to your state
- Payroll tax records
- Mileage and other records for your car
- If you are going to submit expenses for a home business expense, you want measurements of your house and your office space and the records for your utilities, etc. if you are going to submit expenses for a home office. Remember, if you are going to declare a home business expense, the area that you use needs to be set up specifically for that purpose.

You'll want to take copies to leave with your accountant—be sure to keep your originals. In fact, create a duplicate package of the materials to keep for yourself. If he calls with any questions, it's much easier to discuss when you have an exact copy in front of you (versus scrambling for the file that you can't find). Not that you would do that—just speaking from personal experience!

Time Guidelines for Keeping Business Records for the IRS

Protect yourself from troubles with the IRS. Keep all records and documents that pertain to your business for the required time (period of limitations) in an organized manner. Purchase storage boxes at year's end to save required records that are no longer active. Make sure you label the outside of the box noting the fiscal year and a list of its contents.

The following is a recommended list of Time Guidelines for keeping business records for the Internal Revenue Service (IRS). Be sure to ask for specific advice of your personal accountant.

The Period of Limitations with the IRS is usually 3 to 7 years. However, it is important for you to check IRS Publication 583 and your accountant for specific details regarding your business situation, but the table should help with your decisions. IRS Publication 583 is available from www.irs.gov.

Employee records–You should keep all employment tax records for at least four years after the date the tax becomes due or is paid, whichever is later.

Purchase and disposal of assets–all records should be kept for at least three years after disposing of assets.

As you can see from the IRS table below, if you intentionally fail to report significant income or if you file a fraudulent return or fail to file a return, plan to keep your records indefinitely.

Period of Limitations (*see the table below*): This table (created in 2020) is from the IRS website. Remember, rules about taxes are always changing, so be sure to check each year.

IF you . . .	THEN the period is . . .
1. Owe additional tax and situations (2), (3), and (4), below, do not apply to you	3 years
2. Do not report income that you should report and it is more than 25% of the gross income shown on the return	6 years
3. File a fraudulent return	Not limited
4. Do not file a return	Not limited
5. File a claim for credit or refund after you filed your return	Later of: 3 years or 2 years after tax was paid
6. File a claim for a loss from worthless securities or a bad debt deduction	7 years

Next chapter: Everything you didn't want to know about taxes—and more!

7

Everything You Didn't Want to Know About Taxes

And More!

You will want to properly calculate, record and remit your business taxes to the agency that assesses them. Having your system set up correctly will be a blessing when it comes to filling out the reports, reconciling them with your records and answering any audit questions that the government may have.

Sales tax is a tax that you collect from your clients and customers when they make a purchase from you. You then remit the tax to the state. Plan to comply with sales tax requirements, particularly if you sell tangible goods in a state with sales tax. Contact the State Department of Taxation to file a registration form and provide a deposit if necessary. You may find information by 'googling' your state's name followed by 'sales tax.' For example, 'Nevada sales tax.' If you are uncomfortable with computers, your local librarian is glad to provide you with the contact name and address for your state sales tax office.

When you file the application form for a sales tax license or permit, you will be provided with an information package regarding your state's income tax. Basically, it must be charged on all appropriate sales. For instance, in my state, sales tax is charged on goods, but not services.

Your state may charge tax on services as well. Furthermore,

each county and city in a state may charge different amounts, which need to be tracked separately. There are three states that do not charge sales tax: Oregon, New Hampshire and Delaware. Additionally, some states do not charge sales tax on groceries and pharmaceutical products.

Let's describe a shopping event that is familiar to most of us. When we, as consumers, purchase items, the business that we buy from collects sales tax—you have seen that in almost every store that you've ever been in. The business collects the sales tax and remits it to the state (monthly or quarterly, depending on the business). So when you start your business, you have to collect sales tax from your customers on items that you sell and remit it to the state.

Also, the state only collects sales tax on the transaction to the *ultimate or final* consumer. When the business buys inventory for resale purposes at wholesale pricing, it pays no sales tax on the purchase from the distributer, wholesaler or manufacturer. It's only when you sell your inventory at retail to your customers that you collect sales tax.

When you compute the sales tax, you multiple only the taxable amounts by the rate and add it to the total invoice. The taxable amount is the price you are charging the customer. If the merchandise is on sale or discounted, the tax is calculated on the discounted price. For instance, this receipt shows a combination of non-taxable services and taxable goods.:

Sales of Services (non-taxable)	$350.00
Sales of Goods (discounted price)	$200.00
Original Price of Goods $300.00	
Sales Tax (7% x 200.00) =	$14.00
Total Invoice:	$564.00

When recording this sale in your records, the Sales of Goods and the Sales of Services are recorded as income in your separate income accounts. The Sales Tax that you collect is not income and should never be recorded as such. It is not your money; it is not income and it is not recorded as income. It is a liability that your business now owes to the state and an account, Sales Tax Liability, is created to record the amount due to the state. At the end of the month or quarter, depending on your state, you fill out the appropriate form provided by your state agency and remit the income tax that you collected to them along with the form.

If your business needs to collect different tax rates and remit to different agencies, you still only show one rate to the consumer. Using the same example above, and assessing an additional 2% sales tax for a local development requirement, the consumer would then pays 9% of the $200 ($18.00). The business sends to the state $14.00 and remits $4.00 to the development agency.

Sometimes the state allows you a small (a very small) percentage for your efforts in collecting and remitting this tax. This small allowance is considered income and would be recorded as Other Income or Miscellaneous Income. Other states do not provide for a collection allowance. This specific information is shown on the state's remittal form that you must fill out.

When business owners start tracking sales by dividing them into different accounts (tangible goods, services, taxable, nontaxable, different tax rates, etc.), they often begin shortcutting if they are working with a manual system or if their computerized one is not set up properly. This is dangerous and I discuss it in the next section.

Dangerous Sales Tax Shortcuts

In this section we discuss these shortcuts and why, if you use them, you may end up paying more sales tax and possibly more income tax than you should. You'll also learn how to adjust your totals if you do use these shortcuts.

Shortcut #1: Some business owners use systems that do not provide for the separation of sales revenues from sales tax at the time of the sale. These systems record the total amount that was sold, including the sales tax, in an income account. Remember, sales tax is not to be recorded in an income account; it should be recorded in a liability account. As per our discussion in Chapter 3, sales tax liability is a debt because you owe it to the state. You want to know what your sales tax liabilities are on any given day; therefore, it is important to separate the income and the liability portions. Imagine that, by the end of the month, the total recorded as 'income' is quite large and it is now time to remit the sale tax.

> ***Example***: If the total amount recorded in Sales Revenue (income account) is $15,000 and you decide to short cut the process and send 7% tax to the state, you over pay your taxes. Remember, the $15,000 includes the sales income AND the sales tax, so you would be paying 7% on top of the sales tax that you collected. If you pay sales tax on the entire amount of $15,000 you'll pay:
> $15,000 x .07 = $1,050 (sales tax to remit).
>
> If you have used this shortcut, you'll need to use a simple formula for breaking the sales of $15,000 apart into our two accounts: sales income and sales tax due. Divide the total amount by (1+tax rate), or in our example:
>
> $15,000 ÷ 1.07 = $14,018.69 (sales income). We sold $14,018.69–not $15,000; and we collected $981.31 sales tax. To verify: $14,018.69 x .07 = $981.31 (sales tax to remit)
>
> If you delete the extra step of reducing your gross sales income first, you would have overpaid by $68.69. It doesn't seem like much, but every little bit of savings helps when you own your business. Furthermore, you will pay state and Federal income taxes on the incorrect revenues as well.
> ***Shortcut #2***: Some business owners use the total deposits from

their bank statements each month and consider that amount to be their monthly sales. As per our first discussion, this amount includes sales tax. Additionally, the deposits listed on bank statements can come from other sources such as owner's investments, refunds from vendors and reimbursement from overpayments. If you use the total deposited amount on your bank statement as your sales income, you may be overpaying your sales tax liabilities because you might be paying sales tax on deposited monies that are not subject to sales tax.

My clients have denied that they could ever forget that they invested several thousand dollars and would not be neglectful enough to pay sales tax on it—guess again. You are now a busy entrepreneur with other things on your mind, and I've been witness to this mistake repeatedly.

It is important to have a system that can track the sales independently of other deposits including sales tax amounts so that you can prepare your reports properly and remit the correct amount. Furthermore, if you report those full deposits as sales revenues on your sales tax reports, then you inadvertently include them as income on your Federal and state tax returns. The error would be compounded and not only would you pay extra sales tax each month, but extra income tax on your tax returns.

Consumer Use Tax

Consumer use tax is another way for states to raise money. It is similar to Sales Tax and can usually be remitted on the same form in many states—the "Combined Sales and Use Tax Return" (forms may have slightly different names from one state to another). It's easier to understand Use Tax if we understand Sales Tax completely, see above section.

When your business purchases items to USE (in contrast to inventory items for RESALE), you pay sales tax to the store you buy from. However, sometimes we buy from sources that are out-of-state, online, 1-800 numbers, etc. and those businesses do not charge us sales tax. It is then your business' responsibility to pay this sales tax to the state where your business lives. It is this sales tax that is now called 'use tax,' and it is calculated at the same rate that your county's sales tax is calculated.

It is not just businesses that owe use tax. In most states, all consumers must pay use tax if they have not paid sales tax to the business that they purchased goods from. And, technically, if the sales tax is lower in another state than it is in your own state, you are required to send the difference to your state. Some people drive out of state to save money on large purchases (no sales tax), but guess what?–they have to pay the Use Tax to their own state.

Tracking your non-inventory purchases and making sure that the use tax has been paid can be a royal pain in the behind. However, keep in mind that the penalties are severe. Each state's website has complete information about their specific policies and procedures referring to Use Tax. In these times of economic difficulties, it's certain that states will vigorously pursue offenders.

Federal Self-Employment Taxes

In addition to taxes that are attached directly to your sales and purchases, there are other taxes that your business needs to pay. When your company begins to earn a profit, you are responsible for paying self-employment taxes to the Federal government. Let's take a moment to compare this situation to something you're probably already familiar with–working as an employee in a business.

When you are an employee working for a business, the business is required to deduct 7.65% from your gross pay. The business matches the amount in contributions and the total of both these amounts is sent to the Federal government for the Federal Social Security and Medicare systems.

When you are self-employed, you still have to pay these taxes when your business earns net income. Most business owners are subject to this tax, and this expense should be included when making budgeting projections for your business. Normally, these payments are calculated using 15.3% of your net income for the quarter. There are a number of exemptions and reductions involved in the calculations and you should receive expert advice from your accountant when setting up your payment system and calculating your estimates.

The payments are made quarterly—usually on the fifteenth day of the month following the end of the quarter. For instance, if the first quarter is January through March, the quarterly estimate should be paid before April 15th. If you fail to make quarterly estimated payments, the entire amount is due when you calculate your annual income taxes and there will be substantial penalties and interest.

You may find complete and detailed information at http://www.irs.gov/publications/p505, Publication for Tax Withholding and Estimated Tax.

Taxes and Essential Forms for Hiring Employees

Congratulations … you are thinking about hiring your first employee! Your company has grown and you need an extra set of eyes and a pair of friendly hands to help your business continue expanding. Be careful not to hire employees because you think it makes you look good or because you are lonely and would like some excitement in your business. Be sure you need employees and that you can afford them—they are expensive and there is quite a bit of paperwork involved. Make absolutely certain that you budget for the additional expense.

When you hire an employee, there are forms that are essential that you and she need to initially complete. There will be additional payroll taxes and reporting forms for the taxes that are required of your business by the Federal and state governments on a regular basis—usually monthly, quarterly and annually.

If you have not yet obtained an Employer Identification Number (EIN) from the IRS, you want to acquire one prior to hiring employees. This process is free and relatively painless when performed online. Applications by fax and mail take longer. The link can be found at www.IRS.gov. Soon after receiving your EIN number, you will also receive the IRS booklet "Circular E, Employer's Tax Guide." It is a guide that discusses your responsibilities as an employer and provides tax tables for calculating the employee deductions accurately. You want to keep that readily available as reference to answer any of your questions.

Your employees must fill out two required Federal forms in order to be hired. States may also require additional documentation for state agencies. Immediately upon hiring, each employee needs to provide you with two forms of identification and fill out a Federal I-9 Form. Acceptable forms of identification are indicated on the I-9 form and these forms may be found at http://www.uscis. gov. The form ensures that your new employees can legally be hired in the U.S. At one time it was common practice to retain a photocopy of their ID for your records; however due to security cautions, it is not longer advisable to make copies of an employee's identification.

Additionally, they need to complete a Federal W-4 Form (www. IRS.gov), providing their name, address and their withholding status. There are questions regarding marital status and number of dependents. It is important that this form is accurate so that you can deduct Federal and state taxes properly, but be careful not to offer any information about the number of dependents to claim— that's illegal.

Some states check your new hires against a list of child support evaders and you may be required to submit new employee information each quarter to your state. Your state website for businesses provides all the information and any required forms. You may also receive assistance from your local librarian who can assist you in finding the state contact information.

Each employee needs a separate folder in your filing cabinet, and your chart of accounts needs three new accounts: one for payroll expense, another for payroll tax expense and a third for payroll tax liabilities. Any employee discussions regarding pay increases, scheduling changes, workloads, performance evaluations and related forms need to be kept in the employee's file folder. Be sure to receive updated advice about these forms from a human resource professional. You will want to keep these records for at least three years after the termination date of the employee.

Many small businesses choose to hire a payroll services firm for a nominal fee. Even if you choose to do so, you'll still want to be familiar with the calculation of taxes for budgeting and management purposes.

Calculation of Payroll Taxes

The IRS and some states require that you withhold taxes from employees' checks when issuing them. There will be deductions for income taxes, Social Security and Medicare. When you deduct these amounts from the employees' checks, it stays in your checking account until you then remit it to the Federal government. Be sure to remit these funds when required and DO NOT SPEND the money ... it is not yours. The easiest way to pay these monies is to use the online Electronic Federal Tax Payment System (EFTPS). It is quick, easy and safe to use. The money is deducted directly from your checking account and it no longer provides a temptation to spend it to cover other business expenses.

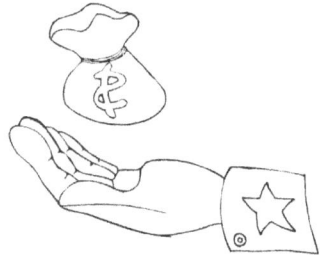

Federal Withholding Taxes (FWH)–To manually deduct the taxes from your employee paychecks, you'll need the Federal "Circular E, Employer's Tax Guide" that has income charts showing you how much to deduct based on the information that the employee filled out in the W-4 form. This is the withholding portion for income taxes and is often abbreviated as FWH or Federal Withholding. You deduct the appropriate amount from the gross wages of your employee on each paycheck. You do not match the Federal withholding portion that is deducted from your employee for income taxes–only your employee has deductions for this tax. Basically, you calculate it, deduct it and hold it temporarily until you transmit it to the IRS.

FICA and Medicare–You also need to deduct 6.2% of the gross wages from each paycheck for Social Security (called FICA–Federal Insurance Contribution Act) and 1.45% of the gross wages for Medicare. Your business needs to match the Social Security and the Medicare portions (also at 6.2% and 1.45% of the gross wages). Your employee pays half for these benefits and your business matches half. For instance, if you deduct $80 from your employee for Social Security and Medicare, your business must also remit an additional $80 with your deposit.

FUTA–In addition, a business pays FUTA (Federal Unemployment Tax Plan) on each employee's first $7,000 of gross earnings. It is paid quarterly or annually depending on the total amount due. For small businesses with annual FUTA payment of less than $500, this tax is usually paid at the end of your fiscal year. You will receive a form from the Federal government. This form is rather complicated as you may receive credit for state unemployment payments. It is recommended that you receive advice from your accountant unless you are very good at following the directions and making the calculations accurately. See www.irs. gov for details.

There are other state taxes for unemployment and disability that your business is required to remit, based on gross payroll amounts, and submit monthly or quarterly. Online resources are a great place to learn about the state requirements. Each of the deposits and reports to the state and Federal governments require an accurate accounting of your payroll and the resulting taxes.

The initial process of calculating payroll can be time consuming and confusing. If you don't have an eye for detail and mathematical computations or the time to concentrate on accuracy, it may be worthwhile to examine the multitude of payroll service companies available. Many businesses use payroll tax service organizations with great success for nominal fees. It pays to compare the different rates and fees—some provide basic payroll; others prepare your reports and submit deposits. Most of the companies process payroll independently of your software system; others have the capability to integrate into your financial software.

One small caveat about selecting a small, local payroll service company. You need to ensure that your tax deposits and your payroll forms are being handled properly and submitted regularly. You must require proof that deposits are made and maintain oversight to protect yourself. Your business is still responsible for all the taxes and any penalties and interest if not paid, or if not paid on time.

Regardless of whether you or another company calculates your payroll and taxes, these amounts need to be integrated into your system and accurately into your accounts.

Recording the Payroll Calculations in Your Accounts

This section helps you visualize how to keep track of your payroll expenses and tax liabilities properly with the use of three new accounts in your chart of accounts: payroll expense, payroll tax expense and payroll tax liabilities.

When you pay your employees, the full amount of the gross payroll expense is recorded into your payroll expense account. When you calculate the deductions from the employees' checks for their portion of the taxes (including FWH, FICA, and Medicare), the deduction is taken from their checks and recorded as a payroll liability. This amount is not your money; it came directly from your employees and needs to go directly to the Federal or state governments.

Additionally, you need to match the FICA and Medicare portions (not the FWH portion), as your business is responsible for an equal amount of these benefits. This amount is a true expense to you and is recorded as a payroll tax expense. You have not quite paid it yet, so you *also* record it as a payroll tax liability. You now owe the employees' portion and your portion. The total amount due should be summarized in the payroll tax liability account.

It may only be five minutes or it may be five days, but this money should remain as a payroll tax liability until you remit the full balance. Either your next step will be to submit the payment of the liability through the EFTPS (Electronic Federal Tax Payment System) or to create a check for this amount. The liability payment is made within a very specific period depending on the size of your payroll.

If you are a new employer and your business has not yet filed Federal 941 forms, then you are a Monthly Schedule Depositor for the first calendar year of your business. Monthly Schedule Depositors should deposit taxes by the 15th of the next month, even if they pay wages every week. As you continue to grow and your payroll increases, you will wish to stay abreast of the time requirements for deposits and due dates at the IRS website.

The Federal 941 forms are the quarterly reports that reconcile your payroll with the deposits that you make each month, and they are due on the last day of the month following the quarter. For instance, the first quarter is January through March. Your 941 form for the first quarter is due on April 30 and shows that you made three deposits for that time period—one for January, another for February and the third for March. The deposits that you made should match the tax amount that you calculate on the Federal 941 forms that is due for the period. If you deposited too much, you can apply the excess to the next quarter by checking a box on the form. If the deposits that you made were short of what you should have paid, you need to send the balance due with the 941 report.

Because employee payroll and benefits are expensive, some business owners choose to use self-employed contractors. A self-employed contractor can provide essentially the same work performance, but (perhaps) at a reduced cost.

Self Employed Contractors Versus Employees

Because payroll taxes and benefits are so expensive, some business owners try to eliminate the responsibility of paying them by hiring self-employed contractors. This is called 'outsourcing' and for many businesses these decisions are appropriate and proper. Your business can pay for specific services without incurring the responsibility and expense of a full-time employee.

However, other business owners maintain their current employees, but try to call them contractors so that the employee has the responsibility of paying the taxes. This is illegal and the IRS will hold the business responsible for the payroll taxes and fines. There is no hard and fast rule when the IRS determines if a contractor is truly an employee, but they examine the answers to several questions. These may help you to determine whether someone working for your business is a contractor or an employee.

If the following answers are no, the person is probably an employee.

- Does the contractor have the ability to earn a profit on her work for you?
- Does the contractor make her services available to the public on a regular and consistent basis?
- When the work is finished, can the contractor leave for the day or week?
- Does the contractor have an investment in significant tools, materials and other equipment when such items are necessary to accomplish the tasks that are customarily provided by the employer?
- Does the contractor have significant investment in facilities when they are necessary to accomplish the task?
- Does the contractor work for more than one firm at a time and accept multiple assignments?
- Does the contractor maintain his or her own business license?

If the following answers are yes, the person is probably an employee.

- Does the contractor work full time and/or exclusively for you, the employer?
- Is the contractor integrated into your business?
- Do you, the employer, require that the work be done in a specific manner and in a specific sequence, allowing the contractor no input in the decision-making?
- Do you, the employer, train the contractor to perform the work?
- Do you, the employer, pay by the hour, week or month (versus paying by the job)?
- Do you, the employer, pay for business and/or travel expenses?
- Does the contractor work only on your business property or designated location?

The full list of questions and discussion can be found at the IRS website. Basically, if it looks like an employee, sounds like an employee and talks like an employee—then it's an employee.

If you are hiring employees and self-employed contractors, then your business is growing substantially and your accounting is becoming more complicated. It's probably time to consider adopting accounting software to make your life easier. With accounting software, you can easily track your employees' and your contractors' time to help evaluate the profitability of each job. You'll discover which jobs are profitable and which ones aren't. In the next chapter, we evaluate the option of converting to a computer accounting software package.

Next Chapter: A Two-Second Click!

8

A Two-Second Click

Computerizing Your Accounting System

Are you ready to move beyond your manual accounting system? Do you want to save time and improve the accuracy of your records and reports? Do you need your reports quickly and regularly? You can have your information at your fingertips—where you need it, when you need it and in the format that you need! Try converting your manual accounting system to a computerized one. A computer software program creates the same reports in the same manner as a manual system, but the math is ensured to be accurate and you can have your reports quickly and easily.

There are a number of inexpensive software programs that are readily available to new business owners and you may wish to take advantage of one—they are a great starting point. You may wish to install a basic software program and learn to use it while your business is small. Software programs that are appropriate to your industry can also help you create, store and retrieve vital information in an accurate and timely fashion. As you begin understanding the basic steps of computerized accounting you'll have financial reports that you'll love.

As you install your software you must protect yourself and your clients from any malicious use of financial information available in your computer files. The easiest way to do this is to provide a security password for your computer and your software programs. A password is

absolutely free and provides an important layer of protection in the event that your computer or your files are stolen or otherwise compromised. Do not share your password with anyone, including your spouse, your partner or your employees. It is important that each person has his or her own password, and setting a new one takes less than 30 seconds. Even if you are receiving accounting help from professionals, create a separate security password for them.

File your user names and passwords in a location that is kept secure from prying eyes, and yet convenient for you. If you forget one, you can locate it readily. Do not jot your password on a yellow sticky note and leave it on your desktop or attached to your monitor.

Most accounting software tracks entries and activity (made intentionally or accidentally) by passwords. This is an internal auditing mechanism that exists in most financial software packages and is intended to protect you and to provide audit reports should you ever need them.

It is essential that you make a backup of your accounting files on a weekly basis, if not more frequently. Make a backup on a separate 'travel' or 'USB drive.' It takes very little effort to back up your files. The time, money and frustration it can save you in the event of a computer malfunction is immeasurable. Store your backup files in a location other than the office in which you have the computer, and preferably off-site. A safety deposit box is a great location for a regular backup. There are also companies that completely back up your computer records daily through Internet access for a nominal fee. The process is automatic and the convenience is great!

Once you make the decision to adopt accounting software, your life will change for the better. Your records will be easier to maintain, and your reports more timely, and you will be able to feel secure and confident that the records you use provide the information you need regarding the performance of your business.

What Software is Available for Accounting?

There are a number of inexpensive software programs and many websites offer a chart showing the comparisons of the features. If you are relatively new to computers and software, you will want a program that is 'user-friendly' and processes information in a manner that is similar to your manual accounting system—something simple to use. Do not over purchase an accounting program, you can always upgrade.

My favorite is QuickBooks Pro® and I've been using it for over twenty years. It provides an integrated business system that includes check writing, bill paying, invoicing, inventory control, estimating, ordering, reconciliations, customized reporting features and technical support. There are several versions of QuickBooks®—the simplest being Simple Start®. This version provides an electronic checking account and gives you the basic tools for getting started in business.

Some new business owners choose to use Quicken® because they have been using it for their personal finances. It was designed for personal finances and also provides an electronic checking account. The terminology is a bit different—for instance, referring to the accounts as categories. Data files from either of the software programs, Quicken® and SimpleStart®, can ultimately be easily imported into the next advanced level, QuickBooks Pro®, with total accuracy.

Other companies sell alternative financial software packages. Some people have used them with success. I just happen to know that the QuickBooks® products are simple to use and straightforward to understand, and you can correct any mistakes easily. They provide an inexpensive tool that works well for most businesses and non-profits.

Regardless of the brand you select, if you start with a simple version, you can learn the basics and then upgrade as your business grows. When you make these upgrades, you may wish to keep a separate backup file or archive of your original file just in case you ever need to reopen it in the old program. Remember, once you've changed your Simple Start® or Quicken® working file into a QuickBooks Pro® working file, you can no longer open that file with Simple Start® or Quicken®–it's always opened with your current software version.

With that said, I must provide a strong recommendation that you obtain professional assistance when you set up your initial company files. Because the software seems relatively easy to use, business owners often get help from family and friends who are not familiar with accounting. It is imperative that the accounts and account types be correctly set up in the chart of accounts. Once your accounts are set up properly and your inventory and services are mapped correctly to the accounts, the reports that you print will help you make wise business decisions. You will love the information that is available at your fingertips, quickly and simply!

Tips for Hiring a Self-Employed Consultant or Bookkeeper

Regardless, of whether you use a manual accounting system or software, there may come a day when you no longer have the time or the interest in taking care of your own weekly recordkeeping and accounting. You may wish to consider hiring an outside contractor, consultant or bookkeeper. In this section are recommendations to consider when discussing possible services.

If you have not yet selected software, choose your consultant first. If you do use software, know what it is and what version and what year it was released. Some independent consultants or bookkeepers only provide services for one software program; others are familiar with many software programs.

Share a little about your company, how you've been using the software and what concerns you're facing–perhaps you need more detailed reports. Instead of your basic financial statements, you may now want to have job profitability reports or a cost accounting system created. Your consultant will also ask how long you've been using the software and if there are major issues that you'd like to address. If appropriate and not too complicated, share with the consultant an example of the specific questions you have. For instance, you might mention that you think your income statement appears to be accurate, but that your balance sheet is not.

If you need to clean up your data due to mistakes, say so. Now is not the time to be shy. As a side note, if you are aware that your data file contains a multitude of mistakes, do not file your tax returns using those numbers. The mistakes made in the first year carry forward into ALL your reports in the future. Several years of mistakes are a challenge to correct. If, after a number of years, these mistakes are ultimately corrected, you may have to adjust tax returns for each of those years. This can be tedious, time consuming and expensive. And, when you choose to correct your data files that span a number of years, you must consult with your tax accountant prior to making corrections.

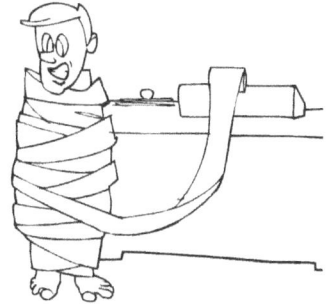

Other questions for you to consider are whether you want to hire the consultant on a regular basis or just to clean up the books and provide education for you and your employees. Let the consultant know if you want to continue taking care of the daily accounting in-house or if you'd like to consider an ongoing relationship with her. Another question to ask yourself as your business grows is, "Do you need CFO (Chief Financial Officer) services?" A CFO who meets with you regularly can certainly help you understand your reports and how to use them to make wise management decisions.

Be sure to ask about fees. They are usually different for a short-term project compared to an ongoing regular service. Many consultants teach for local colleges. Ask if they have classes available that are appropriate for business owners. Not all classes are the same. Some that are more academic in nature with extensive homework may not be the best option for a busy business owner. Other classes are specifically created for business owners and managers, lasting for short periods of time. Some consultants offer teleseminars and coaching for clients, which can be an effective and inexpensive method to learn the skills you need. Be sure to take advantage of all the options. See www.marie-gibson.com for current educational opportunities.

Many contractors have started using written agreements so that everyone is clear about the expectations. Be upfront about discussing the contract or memo of understanding. A memo of understanding is a short document that clarifies everyone's understanding of the relationship—unlike a contract, it is not always binding. If there's something you don't understand, be sure to ask for an explanation. Don't sign an agreement that you haven't read and/or don't comprehend.

Keep the appointments that you schedule with the contractor and practice open communication. She or he is there to help. You'll be delighted to have her simplify your life and create reports you can understand!

Reducing the Potential for Embezzlement

When an owner initially starts hiring employees and contractors, it's usually because the business is growing faster than she can handle by herself and she needs help. On one hand, employees are a blessing; on the other hand, they can be difficult to manage. Occasionally employees or contractors take money and other assets that belong to the business. This form of theft is called embezzlement. Usually embezzlement of funds or assets occurs when the owner is too busy to pay attention to the work and the business doesn't have a proper system in place.

Remember, even the most elaborate system does not totally prevent embezzlement. However, a basic system can go a long way to reduce the potential for a trusted employee to take money. And, yes, it's usually the trusted employee that takes money because that's who we allow access to our money and our accounts.

According to the many stories that I have heard through the years, people who embezzle (for the most part) do not set out to intentionally steal from their friends or employers. They are usually people that are short of cash and just happen to have access to yours. They borrow it for a short time and then pay it back. This may happen repeatedly until the borrower is unable to pay it back. But, guess what? Nobody noticed. You, the owner, didn't notice the borrowing and paying back of funds, and you didn't notice when it wasn't paid back. Hmmm . . . maybe you don't need it right now as badly as the borrower does. And the borrowing continues, usually again with the full intention of paying it back. Unfortunately, at some point in time, the employee or contractor isn't able to repay the money or quits trying because no one questions the missing funds.

Checks and balances–A standard system of 'checks and balances' by a separation of duties should help provide an audit trail of the cash and reduce the possibility of embezzlement. Separation of duties is the specific term that describes assigning different people to jobs that are related to money. It is relatively easy to separate financial duties and it may prevent, or at least reduce, this unapproved 'borrowing' of your money.

Having only one person perform all the accounting responsibilities opens you up to embezzlement more readily than if you have two employees (even part-time) splitting the duties between them. For instance, if one employee is in charge of the cash register every day, the other is in charge of preparing and making the bank deposit. If one person opens the mail and records the payments from your clients and customers, it should be another person that takes them to the bank. If you are unable to split these duties, then you need to oversee the person's work conscientiously.

It is important to look at your records and your reports at least monthly, preferably weekly. Ask questions when you do not understand a transaction. Look at the details of the transactions and the reports. This does not mean that you have to wade through tons of paperwork, but it does mean that you need to make sure that you at least give the appearance of paying attention and pondering over the business' reports.

If your business seems to be earning a profit and yet when you look at your income statement you have a net loss, you may have an embezzlement problem. Or if you are continually fighting cash flow issues on a regular basis, you need to stop whatever you are doing and immediately examine your reports. If you have a number of checks returned by the bank for insufficient funds (NSF funds), do not allow your bookkeeper to brush them under the table. You must at all times understand what is going on in your business and how your reports are a reflection of those transactions.

A big part of your system is the simple appearance of paying attention—of asking questions. Take time to sit with your reports and learn to understand the language they contain. Pay attention to your gut feeling. If your reports aren't accurate, if your employee is constantly scattered and you don't get straight answers from him or her, then you need to delve deeper. Get professional help if you need it—but find the answers to your questions.

There are some specific steps you can take to create a basic system of checks and balances. They are not time consuming, nor are they difficult. They do, however, require you pay attention to your financial processes and system to protect your business and your money.

EMBEZZLEMENT PROTECTION—SIMPLE IDEAS TO HELP YOU CREATE YOUR "CHECKS AND BALANCES"

You can implement some specific steps and tips that will help you create a better system. No system eliminates the possibility of embezzlement completely, but you can reduce your chances by following these simple tips:

1. One simple way of creating a check system, especially if you are not computerized, is to use invoice books and sales receipt pads. Make sure that the books and pads are numbered and assign a specific book to each employee. Account for all of the receipts from the books on a regular basis. That's right; make sure that all of the receipts are there. If there are receipts missing, the employee should know where they are. Receipts in a book like this should never be destroyed. If there's a mistake made on the receipt, it can be voided and approved by you. If you use this simple system in a restaurant, you also know if you're having a problem with customers leaving without paying. If so, you can take action to reduce that problem.

2. Make sure that all employees take their vacation time when appropriate and that he or she takes it in its entirety. An employee that foregoes his or her vacation for the 'sake of the company' may be concerned about leaving and having someone discover his or her trail of embezzlement. He or she will be uncomfortable about another person taking over his or her duties (even temporarily) for the fear of exposure.

3. It's not just money that goes missing–employees can take supplies, inventory and other assets, and this is just as costly. Let employees know that you will not tolerate petty thievery and be sure to set a good example. Make sure that you don't take business assets home for personal use without accounting for them properly, usually as an equity withdrawal. This sets a good example.

4. Check references of prospective employees, even the ones that you know. You may receive interesting information from prior employers that suggests that you shouldn't hire someone. Do not give in against your gut feeling, it doesn't matter how much you desperately need someone to help you.

5. As your company grows and you add more employees, be sure to look at the payroll records occasionally and make sure you recognize all the names of employees.

6. If your business sends out statements to customers and clients, have the return payment sent to a postal address. This limits access to client checks to only the employees that are supposed to have access to them.

7. Make sure that your employee obtains the deposit slips receipt from the bank. Attach the receipt to the appropriate copy in your deposit book. Occasionally, leaf through the copies and make sure that the deposit slip receipt from the bank matches the deposit slip.

8. Send your bank statement to a postal box or to your personal home. If you do not perform the bank reconciliation yourself, at least open the envelope and look at your returned checks. Check the Payee line and make sure that you recognize every payee. If one looks amiss, double-check it. This simple process takes fewer than five minutes a month and reduces the risk of an employee writing checks and paying fake vendors from your business.

9. Sign your bank checks yourself. If your business makes payments with credit cards and debit cards, make sure that you examine the appropriate statements monthly.

10. Do not pre-sign any checks that haven't been filled in. Lock your blank checks in a secured cabinet. Do not leave them lying on a shelf available to any one that walks in.

If you suspect that your employee or contractor is embezzling, make sure that you ask plenty of questions about transactions you don't understand. Do not turn a 'blind eye.' It is your money and you are working hard for it. There are many ways for employees to steal, regardless of how comprehensive your system is. Do not be embarrassed if you find that someone has found ways to work around your system. People are very creative. If you are certain that your employee is stealing from you, contact your accountant immediately. He or she will help you take the next steps in contacting an attorney and the police. Do not hesitate to press charges, even if your business' system has been lax. There is absolutely no excuse for anyone to use their trusted position to embezzle funds, regardless of the simplicity of the business system.

Next Chapter: Odds 'N' Ends!

9

Odds 'N' Ends

More Stuff You Need to Know

Deposits and Down Payments

Recording deposits and down payments may be confusing for business owners. It takes extra precaution to make sure they are recorded correctly, depending on whether your business is receiving them or paying them.

YOUR BUSINESS RECEIVES A DEPOSIT OR DOWN PAYMENT FROM A CUSTOMER

When your customers make a deposit or down payment on a future purchase, record the money as a liability in a deposit or down payment account. This is a liability account type. The money does not yet belong to your business and you may have to return it if the transaction is not completed. Whatever you do, _do not_ record it as income. It will be regarded as income in the future, but you must wait for the completion of the transaction before you move it from the liability account to the income account.

Furthermore, your business pays sales tax when the amount is recorded as income. When the purchase transaction is complete, you move the deposit from the liability account to the income account. This process is called posting a journal entry. The entry should reduce the liability and increase the income. If you have a simple manual system, you record the transaction on the summary sheets in both files (accounts.) If you have a computerized system, you post this transaction in the general journal.

YOUR BUSINESS PAYS A DEPOSIT

When your business submits a deposit or down payment to another business to purchase goods or services, you should record it in your records as a current (short-term) asset. It is not yet an expense–it's called a down payment or a deposit and it is an asset account type because it's your money and you still own it. When the other business completes the sale to you, you move the deposit money from the account and post it to either an expense or asset account, depending on what you purchased.

If the other business does not perform the agreed upon services, they return your cash. If this happens, you make a journal entry to reduce the down payment account and record an increase of cash in your bank account.

Deposit monies can be inactive for quite some time, as it may take awhile for the transactions to be completed. For instance, you may have to pay a deposit for leasing your building. This stays in your records as an asset until the deposit is either returned to you or applied toward your rent expense. You may wish to reconcile your deposits and down payments regularly, especially if your business accepts or remits a lot of them.

Your decision to post the funds as income, expense or asset is based on the completion date of the purchase or sale, or the return of the funds. Regardless of the directional flow of the money, be sure to record the transactions properly to reflect the timing of the transaction.

Business Bartering—Is It Legal?

Bartering is the exchanging of goods and services between two businesses. The process is entirely legal, if you account for the transaction properly. Be sure to include the exchange in your records–don't try to hide it. Once you've agreed on a fair trade, you'll record the transaction in both income and expense accounts at the fair market value.

Because these barter transactions often 'net' or sum to zero, many businesses disregard accounting for them. However, it is important to track the true expenses and true income of your company, even if it doesn't require cash. You want to have accurate income statements and other reports in order to make good management decisions.

As the economy declines, more businesses are bartering in a formal capacity, and exchange companies have opened to facilitate the exchanging transactions. These companies may perform a valuable service; however, you will wish to compare fees for transactions and you may be required to pay the fees in cash or additional goods. These fees would be recorded in an expense account.

To record barter in your records, you'll record the full amount of income that you would have earned. There is no provision or allowance for discounting. You will, however, also record the value of what you received as an expense. For instance, if you trade your consulting time worth $1,000 for a graphics design expert to work on your website, your income is increased by $1,000 and your expenses also increase by $1,000. Record these transactions in each appropriate account–consulting income and web design expense.

In addition to recording the transactions as income and expenses, the IRS may require certain businesses prepare 1099 forms summarizing the barter transactions at the end of the year. See the IRS website for more information.

Depreciation

Depreciation affects an accounting system in two ways. Depreciation is a term used to describe an accounting transaction that prorates the cost of your asset over the period of its useful life span. The proration is used to reflect the reduction in the value of the asset due to wear and tear over the number of years that you'll be using it. The proration posting entry is usually performed monthly, or at least annually.

When you purchase assets, you summarize their cost in your assets on your balance sheet. To depreciate the asset, you write off the depreciation as a depreciation expense and this expense flows into your income statement. Additionally, you post a reduction of value (for the same amount) in the asset account. This reduction in value is usually given the name Accumulated Depreciation. The depreciation amount is deducted from the value of the asset so that the value is reduced every year. The IRS website provides a list of life spans for assets that are to be used for tax purposes.

Example: A copier may last you five years and, if you purchased it for $2,500, you expect its value to decline by $500 for each of the five years. (Divide the cost of the asset by the number of years it's expected to be useful.) For the first year, the decline in value is recorded as $500 in your Depreciation Expense account. The value of your copier is reduced by the $500 and an entry is made in the accumulated depreciation account. The copier's book value is now $2,000. This depreciation amount of $500 is an expense for each of the five years, even though you didn't pay cash for it during the second through fifth year.

MACRS depreciation–The simple method of depreciation just described is called 'straight-line' depreciation. It is used to explain the concept of depreciation in a simple manner, but it is seldom used to actually calculate your depreciation for Federal tax purposes. When your accountant files the tax return for your business, he or she calculates the depreciation in a different manner, maybe using a system called the Modified Accelerated Cost Recovery System (MACRS). This allows for the cost of your asset to be 'written off' or depreciated at a *faster rate* than straight-line allows. By accelerating the rate of depreciation, your depreciation expense is larger each year causing your net income to be lower. This ultimately results in *lower income taxes*.

Remember, as your depreciation expense increases, your accumulated depreciation also increases by the same amount. This causes your asset's book value to be reduced simultaneously. Once your asset's book value is zero, the depreciation expense stops.

Your asset may still have some market value after its book value is zero. If you then sell the asset, you need to 'recapture' the income from this sale and will need your accountant's advice.

As an alternate to depreciation, you may have the option of filing for a 179 Deduction on your tax return, which allows you to write-off large portions of your asset's cost during the year you acquire it. That's why you need to keep track of asset purchases.

This process of depreciation, book value reduction, recapture of income and expensing assets is a complicated subject and requires the assistance of an accountant so that these transactions are reported properly in both your records and tax returns. The IRS Publication 946 details depreciation for tax purposes.

Accrual-Basis versus Cash-Basis Accounting

As you work with your accountant, you may hear the terms cash-basis accounting and accrual-basis accounting and have no idea what they mean; you may even cringe that you have to start understanding complicated accounting concepts. Rest assured … these terms sound worse than they are.

Cash-basis accounting is used to describe the accounting method of recording transactions only when the cash changes hands, and accrual-basis accounting is the method that records transactions when they actually occur, not when the cash ultimately changes hands. Using a couple of examples helps to clarify these subtle and important distinctions.

Many small businesses operate on a cash basis. With a very simple business, products and services are bought and sold. When these items are purchased, the business pays with cash or check and the expense transactions are recorded on this date. When items or services are sold to customers, they pay you with cash, check or credit card immediately and these income transactions are recorded as of that date. A small business with these types of transactions has no Accounts Payable, no Accounts Receivable and, for all practical purposes, very little inventory. This type of accounting, which many small businesses use for years, utilizes a checking account and credit card to record transactions. It is an extremely simplified accounting system.

However, as a business grows, it may begin opening vendor charge accounts (buying items on credit). It may begin allowing customers to pay on credit (remember, these are called terms). It may acquire inventory that carries over from year to year, which continues to grow. These transactions require a more sophisticated accounting system so that the financial statements accurately report the financial position of the company. Accounts Payable and Accounts Receivable accounts need to be created. Inventory asset accounts are created, and these accounts affect the timing that cash goes into, or out of, your checking account. It is this more advanced system that is called accrual-basis accounting.

Transactions in this accrual-basis system are recorded when they actually occur, NOT when the cash comes in or out of the checking account. For instance, if you purchase inventory items with terms, they are recorded in your inventory account and your A/P account, increasing both accounts (you increase your assets and you increase your liabilities at the same time). It may be thirty days, sixty days or longer until you actually pay for these items. When you finally pay for the items, the payment is recorded, reducing the cash in your checking account and also reducing your A/P account. You reduced your checking account by paying, and no longer owe the vendor a debt.

Likewise, if you allow a customer to owe you for services and sales, you record income on the day of the transaction even though you haven't received any money yet. It also is recorded in your A/R account. (Your income increased, your Accounts Receivables increased). When the customer finally pays, entries are made to reduce the A/R account and increase your checking account balance.

If your business has A/R, A/P or inventory, you create an accrual-basis accounting system. For the most part, the IRS requires businesses with inventory to be on an accrual-basis of accounting. If you have been using a simple cash basis and your business grows, ultimately needing an accrual-basis of accounting, you need to file a request form with the IRS to change your basis. Your accountant can help you with the filing of these forms.

Warning: Some businesses purchase inventory and have extensive inventory in the storeroom, yet record these purchases as expenses (perhaps, recorded as a supplies expense). This is inaccurate and will likely cause your net income to be too low and you will not pay adequate Federal income tax. It is imperative that, at some point in time, an adjustment be made for the supplies expense–changing them to inventory items. You will want to receive the assistance of your accountant for this shift in recording.

Next chapter: Budgeting for Profit!

Budgeting For Profit!

Why Else Would You be in Business

A budget is a written financial plan. It is a road map for your business. It shows where you are now, where you are going and how you are going to get there. It also shows how much it will cost and what your income will be along the way. Budgeting is an activity that some business owners shy away from because they think it's too time consuming or too difficult or they think that they can do it in their heads. However, it is not much different than the budgeting you do for your personal life. You have income and you have expenses, and you plan to have some money left over at the end of each month. As you work on your business, you will want to give your full attention to budgeting on a regular basis. Do not shortcut or eliminate this process.

You want to create a written annual budget broken into monthly income and expense areas for planning purposes. This budget can be compared to your actual expenses and your actual income so you can determine how well you forecast for the time period. You may need to adjust your business plans and decisions in the future.

Start-up budget–There are a number of different types of budgets. The two most common are the start-up budget and the operating budget. A start-up budget details the costs that your business requires for starting. It is expense driven and you list every cost you can think of that is required to begin your business, prior to acquiring any income. These expenses include licensing, supplies, advertising, deposits, computers, software, furniture, inventory, printing and all other costs that you incur before you can earn income. Most of these are one-time costs. This budget helps you decide how much money you need to invest or borrow to start your business. This process takes a great deal of research. You'll want to be sure of your expenses–not just guesstimate them.

Operating budget–Your operating budget is based on the regular reoccurring expenses that it takes to run the business each month. Assumptions about your projected income and expenses need to be realistic. These include rent, insurance, telephone, supplies, marketing, memberships, payroll, travel, etc. Sometimes a certain type of expense (for instance, supplies) may be listed in both your start-up budget and your operating budget–and that's fine.

When creating operating budgets, many business owners are able to accurately predict income to a penny–they have a keen sense of knowing their customers. However, they neglect the expense portion of the business, having no idea what is required to earn that very income.

Other business owners know within a penny what their expenses are and yet they are lost when it comes to predicting income. It is imperative to combine both portions of your business so that you have full insight into whether you are making a profit. "Will there be any money left after you pay your expenses?"

I remember helping a client who struggled with her budget. She was never able to create a profit on paper. Yet, she insisted on starting her business, as she was fully convinced that she would be able to make a profit in real life. Guess what? If you are unable to create a profit in a paper budget, it will not materialize in real life. These budgets are the map that you will be following in your business.

If you are already in business and have never created a budget, you'll use your previous income statement as a guide. It helps determine if your business is going to perform similarly. You may also have new products and services and you'll build these plans into your budget. Perhaps, you have a major expansion plan, which requires you to analyze the proposed income and resulting expenses. It is best to capture these numbers on paper through budgeting, prior to expanding.

In the next section we work with budgets from both the expense side and the income side. By understanding the value of each, your ability to run a profitable business is stronger.

The Budgeting Process

If you are a new business owner in the early stages of planning, you may feel more comfortable beginning your research and analysis with the expenses. To begin, make an estimate of your monthly expenses, which includes those costs listed previously: rent, phone, utilities, insurance, payroll (including your own salary), supplies for your office, membership fees, different taxes, advertising and others.

When you have this total, you must be able to earn income at least equal to the expense amount, just to break-even. Break-even is exactly as it sounds—no profit, no loss. If your business provides services, you need to earn the same amount of money as the total of your expenses to break-even. If your income is larger than your expenses, you earn a profit.

Example #1–Service Revenues: The question some business owners neglect to address in the budgeting process is, "How are you going to sell the required amount of services?" If your operating expenses are $5,000 monthly, you need to bring in at least $5,000 monthly in service revenues–just to *break-even*. "HOW is your business going to bring in that income?" Let's delve a little deeper. If you charge $50 an hour, that's one hundred billable hours each and every month. Averaging four weeks in a month, that's twenty-five billable hours each week. Do you have a strong customer base? Are there enough people to sell your services to in your area? How do you continue to bring in these sales each month? If you are just starting, you need to build a customer base either through networking or marketing. Adjust your budget to allow for this start-up phase.

Example #2—Merchandise Sales Revenues: If your business sells merchandise, you'll take into account the cost of the inventory. For instance, if you purchase an item for $10, you'll mark it up to $20. As we discussed earlier (in COGS—cost of goods sold), the $10 is a true cost and needs to be included in your calculations. If your operating expenses are $5,000 monthly, you need to sell at least $10,000 in merchandise. The $10,000 of sales costs your business $5,000 (COGS), leaving you with a margin of $5,000. From this amount, you'll pay for your expenses of $5,000, providing a break-even point for your business.

Then, you focus on your plan to sell $10,000 worth of merchandise. Assuming that you are open 26 days a month, you need to sell $385 each and every day. How many sales do you need to make? What will your average sale look like? For instance, if your customers purchase $50 in an average sale, you need at least eight customers each and every day to purchase that amount. That's over two hundred customers in a month. Assuming that not every customer buys every month, what is your marketing plan to have access to that many customers?

This process of budgeting (backing into your sales, based on your expenses) becomes an easy way to overestimate your sales revenues and income. Business owners are always optimistic about sales and convince themselves that the customers will materialize. It is important to be realistic in all your projections and you may wish to use another form of budgeting. You want to consider how your marketing plan drives clients and customers into your business and what they will purchase from you specifically. From this information, you create your sales and revenues budget.

You begin this type of budgeting by making assumptions about your clients and how often they will purchase from you. This is called a sales forecast or budget. For instance, an Internet business has a customer database of six hundred clients. Each client spends $10 monthly for a newsletter subscription for a total of $6,000. Ten percent of the clients also purchase additional services averaging

$20 per purchase for an additional $1,200. And one percent of the customer base makes a $45 purchase monthly for another $270. This totals $7,470 monthly and could be expected to grow or decline depending on the offerings that the business makes. It is this attention to detail that is important for estimating your income accurately on your budgets.

One more thought about budgets. I've witnessed business owners get caught in the trap of working for free—perhaps, convincing themselves it's just for a month or two. The temporary state becomes permanent when you can't find a way to earn a profit and pay yourself. You and your family may be prepared and able to support the business in this manner for a short time period; however, it is important that, as you budget, you build in money to pay you for your time and effort.

Our last warning question to ask yourself in regards to budgeting for a new business, "Is the net profit enough for you to live on?" In our earlier example, the revenues are $7,470 per month with expenses of $5,000, leaving a monthly net profit of $2,470. This money needs to pay your loans, buy new inventory to expand, purchase new equipment and pay you. Make sure that it's enough to cover these obligations, or you need to re-evaluate your budgets.

Throughout the year, you will want to compare your income statement to your original budget on a regular basis. Analyze the numbers to see where you were accurate and where you need to fine-tune your plans. Revise your next budget to better reflect the true operations of your business. Financial budgeting is one of the most important parts of creating your business plan. With numbers and goals, you will have direction in guiding your business decisions. You must find ways to obtain those eight sales daily that average not just $50 in sales, but $60 and $75.

By watching the numbers, by understanding your financial reports and by comparing your plans and projections with your business performance,

you grow as a business owner and help your business grow as well.

It is my good fortune to be acquainted with many business owners that are growing their businesses. And, every one that has done so, relies on the budgeting and planning and an evaluation process provided to him or her by the numbers. Numbers are their friends and they understand how to read their financial statements, compare their reports with their budgets, make adjustments with wise business decisions and successfully create net profit! You have the right to understand your financial reports. You have the right to make time to budget and compare your budgets to your financial statements. You, too, have the right to have an accounting system that works for you. *Simply, without chaos and with confidence!!*

My best and warmest wishes to each of you as you set up your accounting system using the information in this book. I am confident that if you follow the suggestions made in this book, you too will have **Smart Books. *And remember*–ACCOUNTING 1, 2, 3 FOR BUSINESS OWNERS**.

I am available for additional consulting, workshops and training and may be reached at www.marie-gibson.com.

Warm regards,

Marie Gibson

www.ingramcontent.com/pod-product-compliance
Lightning Source LLC
Chambersburg PA
CBHW071604200326
41519CB00021BB/6859